P9-DBI-895

LAW, CRIME AND LAW ENFORCEMENT

THE MEDICAL MARIJUANA QUESTION AND DEA OPPOSITION

WITHDRAWN

LAW, CRIME AND LAW ENFORCEMENT

Additional books in this series can be found on Nova's website under the Series tab.

Additional E-books in this series can be found on Nova's website under the E-book tab.

PUBLIC HEALTH IN THE 21ST CENTURY

Additional books in this series can be found on Nova's website under the Series tab.

Additional E-books in this series can be found on Nova's website under the E-book tab.

LAW, CRIME AND LAW ENFORCEMENT

THE MEDICAL MARIJUANA QUESTION AND DEA OPPOSITION

CHARLES GABLE
AND
MARCUS FEUERSTEIN
EDITORS

New York

CUYAHOGA COMMUNITY COLLEGE
EASTERN CAMPUS LIBRARY

Copyright © 2013 by Nova Science Publishers, Inc.

All rights reserved. No part of this book may be reproduced, stored in a retrieval system or transmitted in any form or by any means: electronic, electrostatic, magnetic, tape, mechanical photocopying, recording or otherwise without the written permission of the Publisher.

For permission to use material from this book please contact us:
Telephone 631-231-7269; Fax 631-231-8175
Web Site: http://www.novapublishers.com

NOTICE TO THE READER

The Publisher has taken reasonable care in the preparation of this book, but makes no expressed or implied warranty of any kind and assumes no responsibility for any errors or omissions. No liability is assumed for incidental or consequential damages in connection with or arising out of information contained in this book. The Publisher shall not be liable for any special, consequential, or exemplary damages resulting, in whole or in part, from the readers' use of, or reliance upon, this material. Any parts of this book based on government reports are so indicated and copyright is claimed for those parts to the extent applicable to compilations of such works.

Independent verification should be sought for any data, advice or recommendations contained in this book. In addition, no responsibility is assumed by the publisher for any injury and/or damage to persons or property arising from any methods, products, instructions, ideas or otherwise contained in this publication.

This publication is designed to provide accurate and authoritative information with regard to the subject matter covered herein. It is sold with the clear understanding that the Publisher is not engaged in rendering legal or any other professional services. If legal or any other expert assistance is required, the services of a competent person should be sought. FROM A DECLARATION OF PARTICIPANTS JOINTLY ADOPTED BY A COMMITTEE OF THE AMERICAN BAR ASSOCIATION AND A COMMITTEE OF PUBLISHERS.

Additional color graphics may be available in the e-book version of this book.

LIBRARY OF CONGRESS CATALOGING-IN-PUBLICATION DATA

ISBN: 978-1-62417-080-5

Published by Nova Science Publishers, Inc. ✝ New York

CONTENTS

PREFACE

As part of a larger scheme to regulate drugs and other controlled substances, federal law prohibits the cultivation, distribution, and possession of marijuana. No exception is made for marijuana used in the course of a recommended medical treatment. By categorizing marijuana as a Schedule I drug under the Controlled Substances Act (CSA), the federal government has concluded that marijuana has "no currently accepted medical use in treatment in the United States." This book will review the federal government's constitutional authority to enact the federal criminal prohibition on marijuana; highlight certain principles of federalism that prevent the federal government from mandating that states participate in enforcing the federal prohibition; consider unresolved questions relating to the extent to which state authorization and regulation of medical marijuana are preempted by federal law; and assess what obligations, if any, the U.S. Department of Justice (DOJ) has to investigate and prosecute violations of the federal prohibition on marijuana.

Chapter 1 - As part of a larger scheme to regulate drugs and other controlled substances, federal law prohibits the cultivation, distribution, and possession of marijuana. No exception is made for marijuana used in the course of a recommended medical treatment. Indeed, by categorizing marijuana as a Schedule I drug under the Controlled Substances Act (CSA), the federal government has concluded that marijuana has "no currently accepted medical use in treatment in the United States." Yet 16 states and the District of Columbia have decriminalized medical marijuana by enacting exceptions to their state drug laws that permit individuals to grow, possess, or use marijuana for medicinal purposes. In contrast to the complete federal prohibition, these 17 jurisdictions see medicinal value in marijuana and permit the drug's use under certain circumstances.

Although the U.S. Supreme Court has established Congress's constitutional authority to enact the existing federal prohibition on marijuana, principles of federalism prevent the federal government from mandating that the states actively support or participate in enforcing the federal law. While state resources may be helpful in combating the illegal use of marijuana, Congress's ability to compel the states to enact similar criminal prohibitions, to repeal medical marijuana exemptions, or to direct state police officers to enforce the federal law remains limited by the Tenth Amendment.

Even if the federal government is prohibited from mandating that the states adopt laws supportive of federal policy, the constitutional doctrine of preemption generally prevents states from enacting laws that are inconsistent with federal law. Under the Supremacy Clause, state laws that conflict with federal law are generally preempted and therefore void. Courts, however, have not viewed the relationship between state and federal marijuana laws in such a manner, nor did Congress intend that the CSA displace all state laws associated with controlled substances. Instead, the relationship between the federal ban on marijuana and state medical marijuana exemptions must be considered in the context of two distinct sovereigns, each enacting separate and independent criminal regimes with separate and independent enforcement mechanisms, in which certain conduct may be prohibited under one sovereign and not the other. Although state and federal marijuana laws may be "logically inconsistent," a decision not to criminalize—or even to expressly decriminalize—conduct for purposes of the law within one sphere does nothing to alter the legality of that same conduct in the other sphere.

This report will review the federal government's constitutional authority to enact the federal criminal prohibition on marijuana; highlight certain principles of federalism that prevent the federal government from mandating that states participate in enforcing the federal prohibition; consider unresolved questions relating to the extent to which state authorization and regulation of medical marijuana are preempted by federal law; and assess what obligations, if any, the U.S. Department of Justice (DOJ) has to investigate and prosecute violations of the federal prohibition on marijuana.

Chapter 2 - Marijuana is properly categorized under Schedule I of the Controlled Substances Act (CSA), 21 U.S.C. § 801, et seq. The clear weight of the currently available evidence supports this classification, including evidence that smoked marijuana has a high potential for abuse, has no accepted medicinal value in treatment in the United States, and evidence that there is a general lack of accepted safety for its use even under medical supervision.

The campaign to legitimize what is called "medical" marijuana is based on two propositions: first, that science views marijuana as medicine; and second, that the DEA targets sick and dying people using the drug. Neither proposition is true. Specifically, smoked marijuana has not withstood the rigors of science–it is not medicine, and it is not safe. Moreover, the DEA targets criminals engaged in the cultivation and trafficking of marijuana, not the sick and dying. This is true even in the 15 states that have approved the use of "medical" marijuana.[1]

On October 19, 2009 Attorney General Eric Holder announced formal guidelines for federal prosecutors in states that have enacted laws authorizing the use of marijuana for medical purposes. The guidelines, as set forth in a memorandum from Deputy Attorney General David W. Ogden, makes clear that the focus of federal resources should not be on individuals whose actions are in compliance with existing state laws, and underscores that the Department will continue to prosecute people whose claims of compliance with state and local law conceal operations inconsistent with the terms, conditions, or purposes of the law. He also reiterated that the Department of Justice is committed to the enforcement of the Controlled Substances Act in all states and that this guidance does not "legalize" marijuana or provide for legal defense to a violation of federal law.[2] While some people have interpreted these guidelines to mean that the federal government has relaxed its policy on "medical" marijuana, this in fact is not the case. Investigations and prosecutions of violations of state and federal law will continue. These are the guidelines DEA has and will continue to follow.

Chapter 3 - This memorandum provides clarification and guidance to federal prosecutors in States that have enacted laws authorizing the medical use of marijuana. These laws vary in their substantive provisions and in the extent of state regulatory oversight, both among the enacting States and among local jurisdictions within those States. Rather than developing different guidelines for every possible variant of state and local law, this memorandum provides uniform guidance to focus federal investigations and prosecutions in these States on core federal enforcement priorities.

The Department of Justice is committed to the enforcement of the Controlled Substances Act in all States. Congress has determined that marijuana is a dangerous drug, and the illegal distribution and sale of marijuana is a serious crime and provides a significant source of revenue to large-scale criminal enterprises, gangs, and cartels. One timely example underscores the importance of our efforts to prosecute significant marijuana traffickers: marijuana distribution in the United States remains the single largest source of revenue for the Mexican cartels.

Chapter 4 - Over the last several months some of you have requested the Department's assistance in responding to inquiries from State and local governments seeking guidance about the Department's position on enforcement of the Controlled Substances Act (CSA) in jurisdictions that have under consideration, or have implemented, legislation that would sanction and regulate the commercial cultivation and distribution of marijuana purportedly for medical use. Some of these jurisdictions have considered approving the cultivation of large quantities of marijuana, or broadening the regulation and taxation of the substance. You may have seen letters responding to these inquiries by several United States Attorneys. Those letters are entirely consistent with the October 2009 memorandum issued by Deputy Attorney General David Ogden to federal prosecutors in States that have enacted laws authorizing the medical use of marijuana (the "Ogden Memo").

The Department of Justice is committed to the enforcement of the Controlled Substances Act in all States. Congress has determined that marijuana is a dangerous drug and that the illegal distribution and sale of marijuana is a serious crime that provides a significant source of revenue to large scale criminal enterprises, gangs, and cartels. The Ogden Memorandum provides guidance to you in deploying your resources to enforce the CSA as part of the exercise of the broad discretion you are given to address federal criminal matters within your districts.

In: The Medical Marijuana Question ...   ISBN: 978-1-62417-080-5
Editors: C. Gable and M. Feuerstein   © 2013 Nova Science Publishers, Inc.

Chapter 1

MEDICAL MARIJUANA: THE SUPREMACY CLAUSE, FEDERALISM, AND THE INTERPLAY BETWEEN STATE AND FEDERAL LAWS*

Todd Garvey

SUMMARY

As part of a larger scheme to regulate drugs and other controlled substances, federal law prohibits the cultivation, distribution, and possession of marijuana. No exception is made for marijuana used in the course of a recommended medical treatment. Indeed, by categorizing marijuana as a Schedule I drug under the Controlled Substances Act (CSA), the federal government has concluded that marijuana has "no currently accepted medical use in treatment in the United States." Yet 16 states and the District of Columbia have decriminalized medical marijuana by enacting exceptions to their state drug laws that permit individuals to grow, possess, or use marijuana for medicinal purposes. In contrast to the complete federal prohibition, these 17 jurisdictions see medicinal value in marijuana and permit the drug's use under certain circumstances.

---

* This is an edited, reformatted and augmented version of the Congressional Research Service
  Publication, CRS Report for Congress R42398, dated March 6, 2012.

Although the U.S. Supreme Court has established Congress's constitutional authority to enact the existing federal prohibition on marijuana, principles of federalism prevent the federal government from mandating that the states actively support or participate in enforcing the federal law. While state resources may be helpful in combating the illegal use of marijuana, Congress's ability to compel the states to enact similar criminal prohibitions, to repeal medical marijuana exemptions, or to direct state police officers to enforce the federal law remains limited by the Tenth Amendment.

Even if the federal government is prohibited from mandating that the states adopt laws supportive of federal policy, the constitutional doctrine of preemption generally prevents states from enacting laws that are inconsistent with federal law. Under the Supremacy Clause, state laws that conflict with federal law are generally preempted and therefore void. Courts, however, have not viewed the relationship between state and federal marijuana laws in such a manner, nor did Congress intend that the CSA displace all state laws associated with controlled substances. Instead, the relationship between the federal ban on marijuana and state medical marijuana exemptions must be considered in the context of two distinct sovereigns, each enacting separate and independent criminal regimes with separate and independent enforcement mechanisms, in which certain conduct may be prohibited under one sovereign and not the other. Although state and federal marijuana laws may be "logically inconsistent," a decision not to criminalize—or even to expressly decriminalize—conduct for purposes of the law within one sphere does nothing to alter the legality of that same conduct in the other sphere.

This report will review the federal government's constitutional authority to enact the federal criminal prohibition on marijuana; highlight certain principles of federalism that prevent the federal government from mandating that states participate in enforcing the federal prohibition; consider unresolved questions relating to the extent to which state authorization and regulation of medical marijuana are preempted by federal law; and assess what obligations, if any, the U.S. Department of Justice (DOJ) has to investigate and prosecute violations of the federal prohibition on marijuana.

INTRODUCTION

As part of a larger scheme to regulate drugs and other controlled substances, federal law prohibits the cultivation, distribution, and possession of marijuana.[1] No exception is made for marijuana used in the course of a recommended medical treatment. Indeed, by categorizing marijuana as a Schedule I drug under the Controlled Substances Act (CSA), the federal government has concluded that marijuana has "no currently accepted medical use in treatment in the United States."[2]

Yet 16 states and the District of Columbia have decriminalized medical marijuana by enacting exceptions to their drug laws that permit individuals to grow, possess, or use marijuana for medicinal purposes.[3] In contrast to the complete federal prohibition, these 17 jurisdictions see medicinal value in marijuana and permit the drug's use under certain circumstances. Such inconsistencies in federal and state law would generally evoke the constitutional principle of preemption—potentially resulting in a conclusion that because the states permit conduct that the federal government has expressly prohibited, such laws are void as in conflict with the "supreme law of the land."[4] This, however, has not been the case. State laws that exempt from state criminal sanctions the cultivation, distribution, or possession of marijuana for medical purposes have generally not been preempted by federal law.

This unique interplay between state and federal law has led to a seemingly incongruous situation in which both the federal criminal prohibition on marijuana and state medical marijuana exemptions coexist. Accordingly, a resident of California who uses marijuana for medical purposes in compliance with California law is nonetheless simultaneously in violation of federal law and potentially subject to prosecution by federal authorities. Such prosecutions, however, are rare. The federal government has limited resources to draw upon in investigating and enforcing federal drug laws.[5] As a consequence, the Obama Administration has formally suggested that it will not prosecute individuals who use medicinal marijuana in a manner consistent with state laws.[6]

The legal anomaly that defines the use of medical marijuana in the United States raises a number of important constitutional questions—some of which have been answered by the U.S. Supreme Court, but many of which remain unresolved. This report will review the federal government's constitutional authority to enact the federal criminal prohibition on marijuana; highlight certain principles of federalism that prevent the federal government from mandating that states participate in enforcing the federal prohibition; consider unresolved questions relating to the extent to which state authorization and regulation of medical marijuana are preempted by federal law; and assess what obligations, if any, the U.S. Department of Justice (DOJ) has to investigate and prosecute violations of the federal prohibition on marijuana.

LEGAL LANDSCAPE: FEDERAL AND STATE LAWS

Prior to considering the significant constitutional questions associated with the interplay between state and federal laws in the context of medical marijuana, the following section provides a description of the CSA and a brief discussion of common characteristics found within the wide variety of state medical marijuana laws that have been enacted across the country.

Federal Law

Enacted in 1970, the CSA establishes a statutory framework through which the federal government regulates the lawful production, possession, and distribution of controlled substances.[7] The CSA places various plants, drugs, and chemicals (such as narcotics, stimulants, depressants, hallucinogens, and anabolic steroids) into one of five schedules based on the substance's medical use, potential for abuse, and safety or dependence liability.[8] Further, the act requires persons who handle controlled substances or listed chemicals (such as drug manufacturers, wholesale distributors, doctors, hospitals, pharmacies, and scientific researchers) to register with the Drug Enforcement Administration (DEA) in DOJ, which administers and enforces the CSA.[9] Registrants must maintain detailed records of their respective controlled substance inventories, as well as establish adequate security controls to minimize theft and diversion.[10]

Marijuana is currently categorized as a Schedule I controlled substance, and is therefore subject to the most severe restrictions contained within the CSA. Schedule I drugs have "a high potential for abuse" and "no currently accepted medical use in treatment in the United States," and lack "accepted safety for use of the drug [] under medical supervisions."[11] Pursuant to the CSA, the cultivation, distribution, or possession of marijuana is a federal crime.[12] Although various factors contribute to the ultimate sentence received, the mere possession of marijuana generally constitutes a misdemeanor subject to up to one year imprisonment and a minimum fine of $1,000.[13] The cultivation or distribution of marijuana, or the possession of marijuana with the intent to distribute, on the other hand, is subject to more severe penalties. Such conduct generally constitutes a felony subject to as much as five years imprisonment and a fine of up to $250,000.[14]

Although individuals who use medical marijuana in compliance with state law are still in violation of federal law and subject to prosecution by federal authorities at any time, the Obama Administration has announced an informal policy that suggests a federal prosecution in that situation would be unlikely. In an October 19, 2009, memorandum, Deputy Attorney General David W. Ogden provided guidance to federal prosecutors in states that have authorized the use of medical marijuana.[15] Citing a desire to make "efficient and rational use of its limited investigative and prosecutorial resources," the memorandum stated that while the "prosecution of significant traffickers of illegal drugs, including marijuana ... continues to be a core priority," federal prosecutors "should not focus federal resources [] on individuals whose actions are in clear and unambiguous compliance with existing state laws providing for the medical use of marijuana."[16] The memorandum made clear, however, that "this guidance [does not] preclude investigation or prosecution, even where there is clear and unambiguous compliance with existing state law, in particular circumstances where investigation or prosecution otherwise serves important federal interests."[17]

Responding to an increase in the "commercial cultivation, sale, distribution, and use of marijuana for purported medical purposes," DOJ released a subsequent memorandum in 2011 drawing a clear distinction between the potential prosecutions of individual patients who require marijuana in the course of medical treatment and "commercial" dispensaries.[18] After noting that several jurisdictions had recently "enacted legislation to authorize multiple large-scale, privately operated industrial marijuana cultivation centers," DOJ attempted to clarify the scope of the Ogden Memorandum:

> The Ogden memorandum was never intended to shield such activities from federal enforcement action and prosecution, even where those activities purport to comply with state law. Persons who are in the business of cultivating, selling or distributing marijuana, and those who knowingly facilitate such activities, are in violation of the [CSA] regardless of state law. Consistent with resource constraints and the discretion you may exercise in your district, such persons are subject to federal enforcement action, including potential prosecution.[19]

The memorandum clearly communicated that individuals operating or "facilitating" medical marijuana dispensaries, even if operated in compliance with state law, continue to be targets for federal prosecution. As a result, the last two years have seen a reported increase in the number of federal DEA raids on dispensaries and marijuana farms and the subsequent prosecutions of those who own and operate marijuana distribution facilities.[20] Additionally, a number of states have abandoned legislative proposals to expand their medical marijuana programs, at least partly as a result of warnings from U.S. Attorneys that the DOJ will "vigorously" enforce the CSA against those who participate in the unlawful manufacturing or distribution of marijuana, regardless of whether such activity is licensed under state law.[21]

State Laws

All 50 states and the District of Columbia have criminalized the recreational use of marijuana.[22] However, beginning with California in 1996, a number of states have decriminalized the use of marijuana for medicinal purposes or exempted qualified users from sanctions imposed under state law. Today, 16 states and the District of Columbia have enacted provisions that, in various ways, exempt qualified individuals[23] from state criminal prosecution and various state civil penalties for marijuana-related offenses.[24] Although these laws vary widely in their approaches to medical marijuana, there are a number of common characteristics that appear to adhere to these laws. First, in order for an individual to legally use medical marijuana, the drug must have been recommended by a physician for use in treating a diagnosed medical condition.[25] All states but California require that this recommendation be in writing.[26] Most states also require potential users to register with the state.[27] Upon registration, states will often provide the user with a registration card so that the individual can be identified as a qualified user of medical marijuana.[28] Additionally, all states but California limit the quantity of marijuana that a patient may possess at any one time, and most states have laws limiting the manner and place in which a qualified individual can use the drug.[29]

Although these 17 jurisdictions have established a scheme by which qualified individuals may legally possess and use marijuana for medicinal purposes under state law, qualified users in some jurisdictions lack a legal avenue to obtain adequate quantities of the drug. Some states permit users to grow their own marijuana, while others license third-party private persons or entities to cultivate and distribute the drug to qualified individuals through state-licensed and -regulated dispensaries.[30] California has also authorized patients and caregivers to collectively grow marijuana in "cannabis cooperatives."[31] In those states where supply is limited, however, many medical marijuana users are forced to acquire the marijuana they are permitted to possess and use through the black market.[32]

A SERIES OF CONSTITUTIONAL QUESTIONS

The unique inconsistencies between federal and state approaches to medical marijuana give rise to a series of important constitutional questions. First, is it within Congress's power to prohibit the production, possession, and distribution of marijuana? Second, to what extent can the federal government direct states to adopt similar laws or enforce the federal prohibition? Third, to what extent are state attempts to authorize and regulate medical marijuana preempted by federal law? And finally, what obligation, if any, does DOJ have to enforce the federal prohibition?

Is It within Congress's Power to Prohibit the Production, Possession, and Distribution of Marijuana?

The U.S. Supreme Court considered the reach of Congress's Commerce Clause authority and the constitutionality of the CSA in *Gonzales v. Raich*.[33] *Raich* involved a challenge to the federal marijuana prohibition brought by Angel Raich and Diane Monson after agents of the federal DEA seized and destroyed marijuana plants that Monson had been cultivating for medical purposes consistent with California law. The respondents argued that the CSA's "categorical prohibition," as applied to the "intrastate manufacture and possession of marijuana for medical purposes," exceeded Congress's authority under the Commerce Clause, and, therefore, could not serve as the basis for their prosecution.[34] The Court rejected this argument, and clearly held that the federal prohibition was within Congress's constitutional authority.

In a 6-3 decision, the Court upheld Congress's power to prohibit even the purely intrastate cultivation and possession of marijuana. Relying heavily on its 1942 decision of *Wickard v. Filburn*, the Court held that prior precedent had "firmly establish[ed] Congress'[s] power to regulate purely local activities that are part of an economic 'class of activities' that have a substantial effect on interstate commerce."[35] In enacting the CSA, Congress had sought to regulate the supply and demand of controlled substances, including marijuana. Consistent with that objective, Congress had rationally concluded that "leaving home-consumed marijuana outside federal control" would have a "substantial effect on supply and demand in the national market" for marijuana.[36] The Court noted that even small amounts of marijuana grown at home— though intended for personal medicinal use—would likely be diverted into the national market and frustrate Congress's goal of strictly controlling overall supply.[37] Thus, in enacting the federal prohibition on marijuana production, possession, and distribution, Congress was acting "well within its authority to 'make all Laws which shall be necessary and proper' to 'regulate commerce ... among the several states.'"[38]

For purposes of this report, it is important to note that the Court's opinion in *Raich* dealt only with the question of whether the Commerce Clause permitted Congress to prohibit the wholly intrastate possession and use of marijuana. The Court did not consider the question of whether the California law, which permitted the use of marijuana for medicinal purposes, was preempted by the CSA. The Court noted only that respondents' compliance with state law in cultivating marijuana had no impact on the scope of Congress's power under the Commerce Clause, as "[i]t is beyond peradventure that federal power over commerce is 'superior to that of the States to provide for the welfare or necessities of their inhabitants,' however legitimate or dire those necessities may be."[39]

May the Federal Government Direct the States to Adopt Similar Laws or to Enforce the Federal Prohibition?

Although *Raich* established Congress's constitutional authority to enact the existing federal prohibition on marijuana, principles of federalism prevent the federal government from mandating that the states support or participate in enforcing the federal law. While state resources may be helpful in combating the illegal use of marijuana, Congress's ability to compel the states to enact similar criminal prohibitions, to repeal medical marijuana exemptions, or to direct state police officers to enforce the federal law remains limited. The Tenth Amendment likely prevents such an intrusion into state sovereignty.

The Tenth Amendment provides that the "powers not delegated to the United States by the Constitution, nor prohibited by it to the States, are reserved to the States respectively, or to the people."[40] Initially, the Supreme Court interpreted the Tenth Amendment as establishing that certain "core" state functions would be beyond the authority of the federal government to regulate.[41] The Court's interpretation of the Tenth Amendment soon shifted, however, from protecting "core" state functions to preventing the federal government from "commandeering" state government.[42] In *New York v. United States*, http://www.crs.gov/pages/Reports.aspx?PRODCODE= RL30315&Source=search - fn118#fn118the Court struck down a federal statute that had mandated that states either develop legislation on how to dispose of all low-level radioactive waste generated within their borders, or be forced to take title to such waste and become responsible for any financial consequences.[43] The Court found that although Congress had the authority under the Commerce Clause to regulate low-level radioactive waste, it had only the power to regulate the waste directly—Congress could not require that the states perform the regulation rather than regulate the waste directly itself. In effect, Congress could not "commandeer" the legislative process of the states.[44]

Nor may Congress "commandeer" state executive branch officers for purposes of carrying out or enforcing federal law. In *Printz v. United States*, the Supreme Court invalidated a provision of the Brady Handgun Violence Prevention Act that had required that state police officers conduct background checks on prospective handgun purchasers within five days of an attempted purchase.[45] The Court held that the provision constituted an unconstitutional "commandeering" of state officers and, like a commandeering of the legislature, was outside of Congress's power and a violation of the Tenth Amendment.[46]

Consistent with *New York v. United States* and *Printz*, the federal government is prohibited from commandeering state legislatures or state executive officials by mandating that states enact certain legislation or implement or enforce a federal law.[47] Given these restrictions, Congress may not statutorily direct that states enact complete prohibitions on marijuana or repeal existing exemptions for medical marijuana. Nor may Congress direct that state police officers enforce the marijuana provisions of the CSA. Congress may, however, be able to persuade states to support the federal policy by conditioning the receipt of federal funds upon the state enacting legislation consistent with the CSA.[48] In addition, states may voluntarily alter their own laws or enforce federal laws, but they cannot be made to do so by the federal government.[49]

To What Extent Are State Medical Marijuana Laws Preempted by Federal Law?

Even if the federal government is prohibited from mandating that the states adopt laws supportive of federal policy, the constitutional doctrine of preemption generally prevents states from enacting laws that are inconsistent with federal law. Thus, the federal government typically stands on much stronger constitutional footing when it attempts to stop a state action than when it attempts to force a state to act.

At first glance, it would appear that a state law that permits an activity expressly prohibited by federal law would necessarily create a legal "conflict" between state and federal law. Under the Supremacy Clause, state laws that conflict with federal law are generally preempted and therefore void.[50] Courts, however, have not viewed the relationship between state and federal marijuana laws in such a manner, nor did Congress intend that the CSA displace all state laws associated with controlled substances.[51] Instead, the relationship between the federal ban on marijuana and state medical marijuana exemptions must be considered in the context of two distinct sovereigns, each enacting separate and independent criminal regimes with separate and independent enforcement mechanisms, in which certain conduct may be prohibited under one sovereign and not the other. Although state and federal marijuana laws may be "logically inconsistent," a decision not to criminalize—or even to expressly decriminalize—conduct for purposes of the law within one sphere does nothing to alter the legality of that same conduct in the other sphere.

Preemption is grounded in the Supremacy Clause of Article VI, cl. 2, which states that "[t]he Constitution, and the Laws of the United States which shall be made in Pursuance thereof; and all Treaties made, or which shall be made, under the Authority of the United States, shall be the supreme Law of the Land."[52] The Supremacy Clause, therefore, "elevates" the U.S. Constitution, federal statutes, federal regulations, and ratified treaties above the laws of the states.[53] As a result, where a state law is in conflict with a federal law, the federal law must prevail. There is, however, a presumption against federal preemption when it comes to the exercise of "historic police powers of the States."[54] State medical marijuana laws have generally been accorded this presumption, as they are enacted pursuant to traditional state police powers in defining criminal conduct and regulating drugs and medical practices.

Although there is "no one crystal clear distinctly marked formula" for determining whether a state law is preempted by federal law, the Supreme Court has established three general classes of preemption: express preemption, conflict preemption, and field preemption.[55] In each instance, however, "the question of preemption is one of determining congressional intent."[56] Express preemption exists where the language of a federal statute explicitly states the degree to which related state laws are superseded by the federal statute.[57] Where, in contrast, Congress does not articulate its view as to a statute's intended impact on state laws, a court may *imply* preemption if there is evidence that Congress intended to supplant state authority.[58] Preemption is generally implied in two situations. First, under conflict preemption, a state law is preempted "where compliance with both federal law and state regulations is a physical impossibility ... or where state law stands as an obstacle to the accomplishment and execution of the full purposes and objectives of Congress."[59] Thus, where one cannot simultaneously comply with both state and federal law, or where the state law directly frustrates the purpose of a federal law, the state law is preempted. Second, under field preemption, a state law is preempted where a "scheme of federal regulation is so pervasive as to make reasonable the inference that Congress left no room for the States to supplement it...."[60]

The CSA contains a statutory preemption provision that expressly articulates Congress's intent as to the relationship between state and federal law and the extent to which the latter displaces the former. Section 903 states:

> No provision of this subchapter shall be construed as indicating an intent on the part of the Congress to occupy the field in which that provision operates, including criminal penalties, to the exclusion of any State law on the same subject matter which would otherwise be within the authority of the State, *unless there is a positive conflict between that provision of this subchapter and that State law so that the two cannot consistently stand together.*[61]

The CSA's preemptive effect is therefore limited to only those state laws that are in "positive conflict" with the CSA such that the two "cannot consistently stand together."[62] Notably, the provision clarifies that Congress did not intend to entirely occupy the regulatory field concerning controlled substances or wholly supplant traditional state authority in the area. Indeed, Congress expressly declined to assert field preemption as grounds for preempting state law under the CSA. Arguably, then, the preemptive effect of the CSA is not as broad as congressional authority could have allowed. States remain free to pass laws relating to marijuana, or other controlled substances, so long as they do not create a "positive conflict" with federal law. In interpreting this provision, courts have generally established that a state medical marijuana law is in "positive conflict" with the CSA if it is "physically impossible" to comply with both the state and federal law, or where the state law "stands as an obstacle to the accomplishment and execution of the full purposes and objectives of Congress."[63]

CSA Preemption as Applied to State Medical Marijuana Exemptions

Both federal and state courts have consistently held that a state's decision to exempt certain classes of individuals from the state prohibition on marijuana by permitting the drug's use for medicinal purposes does not create a "positive conflict" with federal law. A mere exemption from state prosecution neither (1) makes it "impossible to comply" with both state and federal law nor (2) "stands as an obstacle" to the execution of Congress's objectives.

The "impossibility" prong of conflict preemption has traditionally been viewed very narrowly. The Supreme Court has consistently held that there is no basis to imply impossibility preemption where a state simply *permits* what the federal government *prohibits*.[64] So long as an individual is not compelled to engage in conduct prohibited by federal law, then simultaneous compliance with both laws is not impossible.[65] In the medical marijuana context, an individual can comply with the CSA and a state medical marijuana exemption by refraining from the use of marijuana altogether. Under established precedent, it would appear that the federal prohibition on marijuana would only preempt a state medical marijuana law under the impossibility prong of conflict preemption if the state law *required* individuals to use medical marijuana. State laws, of course, contain no such mandate.

The second prong of the conflict preemption analysis is broader in scope. State laws may be deemed to be in conflict with federal law if the state law "stands as an obstacle to the accomplishment and execution of the full purposes and objectives of Congress."[66] In applying this test, the Supreme Court has stated that a reviewing court must consider congressional intent and the "purposes and objectives" of the federal statute as a whole.[67] "If the purpose of the act cannot otherwise be accomplished," the Court has held, then "the state law must yield to the regulation of Congress ..."[68] Additionally, the Court has established that in areas of traditional state concern—an area within which medical marijuana laws likely fall—there exists a presumption against preemption.[69] In these areas, a more "significant" conflict may be required before a state law constitutes an obstacle to the achievement of the federal goal.[70]

Courts have generally viewed state medical marijuana exemptions as having only a limited impact on the federal government's ability to achieve its purpose of combating the use of marijuana pursuant to the CSA. An exemption from prosecution under state law does not obstruct the federal government's ability to investigate and prosecute an individual for a violation of federal law.[71] Federal courts have consistently held that compliance with state medical marijuana laws is no defense, and provides no immunity to a federal criminal prosecution under the CSA.[72] Indeed, in hearing a prosecution under federal law, at least one federal court has gone so far as to exclude the introduction of any evidence relating to the defendant's compliance with state medical marijuana provisions.[73]

While an argument can be made that the decriminalization of medical marijuana under state law represents an "obstacle to the accomplishment ... of the full purposes and objectives of Congress" by creating confusion as to the permissible uses of marijuana, it is not the case that the federal objectives "cannot otherwise be accomplished" in the face of state medical marijuana exemptions.[74] The federal government is still free to expend its own resources to implement and enforce its own law. Moreover, if a state decision to not criminalize conduct otherwise prohibited by federal law qualified as an obstacle to the accomplishment of federal objectives, then obstacle preemption would effectively amount to an impermissible "license to commandeer state or local resources" by denying states the ability to treat certain conduct differently than the federal government.[75]

CSA Preemption as Applied to State Authorizations of Medical Marijuana

With most state medical marijuana exemptions surviving preemption challenges, various states have utilized the resulting momentum to attempt to exert increased state control over the use of medical marijuana within their borders. As a result, some state laws have evolved from merely exempting qualified individuals from prosecution under state drug laws, to affirmatively authorizing and regulating the use of medical marijuana. For example, whereas California's initial medical marijuana law only decriminalized the use of marijuana for medicinal purposes, the state expanded its law in 2003 under the Medical Marijuana Program Act.[76] The law required that the California Department of Public Health establish a voluntary registration and identification system, under which all California counties were required to issue state identification cards to qualified applicants.[77] The law also authorized qualified individuals and primary caregivers to possess up to 8 ounces of marijuana and 6 mature marijuana plants—a provision that was later struck down by the California Supreme Court.[78] Moreover, California now permits the formation of cooperatives through which qualified individuals can cultivate and distribute marijuana.[79]

Although it is difficult to determine the extent to which states can legalize and regulate medical marijuana, laws that exceed a decision not to criminalize specific conduct, and instead actively authorize the use of marijuana in contravention of the CSA, would appear to raise more stark preemption concerns. For example, a state law that attempted to immunize its citizens from federal prosecution would be preempted as a direct obstacle to the accomplishment of federal objectives. So, too, would a state law that sought to protect its citizens from the consequences of marijuana use, such as potential disqualification from public housing, under other federal statutes.[80] Additionally, a strong argument can probably be made that if a state were to enact a law through which the state itself cultivated and distributed marijuana to qualified individuals, such a law would also be preempted.[81] Whether other, less intrusive, state laws may also be preempted remains uncertain.

It does not appear that any federal court has engaged in a substantial discussion of the preemption issues associated with these increasingly expansive state laws.[82] However, in order to highlight the difficulty in delineating the preemptive scope of the CSA, it may be helpful to consider two state cases reviewing the California and Oregon state registration and identification card programs. These laws permit a qualified individual to register with the state and receive an identification card that is used to identify the individual as one who is permitted to cultivate or possess marijuana.[83] In analyzing whether this type of law is preempted by the CSA, the California and Oregon courts have reached very different results.

State-Issued Identification Card Program Not Preempted

In *County of San Diego v. San Diego Norml*, a California appellate court upheld the registration and identification card provisions of the California Medical Marijuana Program Act (MMPA).[84] Challenging the law, San Diego County argued that the provisions of the MMPA which required the county to issue identification cards to qualified patients and primary caregivers were preempted by the CSA and therefore without effect.[85]

In considering the preemption issue, the California court first attempted to define the preemptive scope of the CSA. Interpreting Section 903 of the CSA, the court concluded that Congress had demonstrated its intent to reject both express and field preemption—leaving only conflict preemption as sufficient to preempt a state marijuana law.[86] Notably, after considering the previously discussed "impossibility" and "obstacle" prongs of conflict preemption, the court concluded that the language of the CSA suggested that Congress "did not intend to supplant all laws posing some conceivable obstacle to the purposes of the CSA."[87] Thus, the court rejected the application of "obstacle" preemption under the CSA and held that a state law should only be preempted if it were impossible to simultaneously comply with both state and federal law.

Although determining that obstacle preemption was not applicable under the CSA, the court went on to hold that even if Congress had intended to preempt state laws that made compliance with federal law impossible or that represented an obstacle to the achievement of federal objectives, the California identification laws would still not be preempted under either standard.[88] In reaching this conclusion, the court noted that the identification cards did not "insulate the bearer from federal laws," nor did the card "imply the holder is immune from prosecution for federal offenses."[89] The identification cards, the court reasoned, instead represented a "mechanism" by which California law enforcement officers could efficiently identify those individuals who are exempted from prosecution under California law for their use of marijuana.[90]

State-Issued Identification Card Program Preempted

Contrary to the California holding, in *Emerald Steel Fabricators v. Bureau of Labor and Industries*, the Oregon Supreme Court concluded that similar identification card provisions in the Oregon Medical Marijuana Act were in "positive conflict" with the CSA and therefore preempted.[91] Under Oregon law, the state issues qualified individuals identification cards that authorize the individual to "engage in the medical use ... of marijuana" without the threat of state prosecution.[92] The challenge to the law arose in the context of an employment discrimination claim in which an employee, who had obtained an identification card due to a medical condition, was allegedly discharged for admitting that he used marijuana.[93] Oregon law requires that employers "make reasonable accommodations" for an employee's disability as long as such an accommodation does not impose an undue hardship upon the employer.[94] However, the law is to be interpreted consistently with the federal Americans with Disabilities Act, which does not afford protections for employees "currently engaged in the illegal use of drugs."[95] Although the employee's use of marijuana was legal under state law, the employer argued that the medicinal use of marijuana remains illegal under federal law and that "to the extent that [Oregon law] affirmatively authorizes the use of medical marijuana, federal law preempts that subsection ..."[96]

Unlike the California court, the Oregon Supreme Court concluded that if a state law fell within either the "impossibility" prong or the "obstacle" prong of the conflict preemption analysis, then the state law would be preempted by the CSA.[97] Noting that the Supreme Court has applied the impossibility prong of the analysis "narrowly," the court first determined that an individual could simultaneously comply with both the state and federal law by refraining from the use of marijuana.[98] However, in turning to the obstacle prong, the court held that because the Oregon law "affirmatively authorized the use of medical marijuana," it was preempted by the CSA. The court reasoned that while the law did not prevent the federal government from enforcing its own laws against Oregon users, by "affirmatively authorizing a use that federal law prohibits," the Oregon law "stands as an obstacle to the implementation and execution of the full purposes and objectives of the Controlled Substances Act."[99] Although the court concluded that the state provisions that exempted medical marijuana users from criminal liability were within the states' authority and beyond the reach of Congress under the Tenth Amendment, the licensing provision—which authorizes an individual with an identification card to engage in the use of marijuana—was distinguishable.[100] "There is no dispute," held the court, "that Congress has the authority under the Supremacy Clause to preempt state laws that affirmatively authorize the use of medical marijuana."[101]

County of San Diego and Emerald Steel display the apparent ambiguities associated with delineating the degree to which states can address medical marijuana within their borders. These cases highlight a number of important questions that may play a significant role in how other courts approach these preemption questions. First, will other courts adopt the Oregon Supreme Court's distinction between a permissible "exemption" and an impermissible "authorization"?[102] If so, the consequences of such an approach could be significant. Second, should state licensing laws be characterized as an affirmative state authorization to use marijuana, or merely a mechanism by which state law enforcement officers can identify a specific class of individuals who qualify for the state medical marijuana exemption? These questions, and others, remain unresolved. However, even if state laws were not preempted, the growth of state medical marijuana laws will likely still be limited by the degree to which the federal government is willing to prosecute violations of the CSA.

Liability for State Officials?
It should be noted that state laws that provide a mechanism by which state officials who participate in helping qualified individuals gain access to marijuana may theoretically expose those state officials to federal criminal liability. It is not only individuals who possess, produce, or distribute marijuana who are subject to federal sanctions, but also those who conspire,

aid and abet, or assist in that proscribed conduct.[103] Take for example, state laws that require state officials to return marijuana improperly seized from a qualified individual.[104] Theoretically, the action of returning that marijuana would qualify as a felony distribution of marijuana under the CSA. Although the CSA contains language that may act to protect state officials, the precise impact of the provision remains unclear. Section 885 provides that "no civil or criminal liability shall be imposed ... upon any duly authorized officer of any state ... who shall be lawfully engaged in the enforcement of any law ... relating to controlled substances."[105] This provision may provide protections for state officials carrying out state-directed actions that are in contravention of the CSA.[106]

In contrast, however, the U.S. Attorneys for the Eastern and Western Districts of Washington State have expressly noted that state officials could be subject to prosecution under federal law for carrying out aspects of a state medical marijuana program that violates the CSA.[107] In response to a request for DOJ's position on a proposed expansion to the medical marijuana laws of Washington State, these U.S. Attorneys suggested that "state employees who conducted activities mandated by the Washington legislative proposals would not be immune from liability under the CSA."[108] The letter reportedly played a role in the governor's decision to veto the proposal.

The state of Arizona recently asked a federal district court to resolve the state officer immunity question. Partially out of concern for the potential criminal liability of state employees who implement state law, the governor of Arizona sought guidance from the Arizona United States Attorney's Office on whether the Arizona Medical Marijuana Act created a "safe harbor" from federal prosecution under the CSA. Although not referencing state employees specifically, the U.S. Attorney for the District of Arizona responded with a letter informing the governor that "growing, distributing, and possessing marijuana violates federal law no matter what state law permits," and that "compliance with state law does not create a 'safe harbor.'"[109]

The state filed suit in the U.S. District Court for the District of Arizona, asking the court for a declaratory judgment as to whether the state law created a safe harbor for state officials under the CSA. Without reaching the merits, the court dismissed the claim as unripe, holding that the state could not show that officials were "subject to a genuine threat of imminent prosecution."[110] In reaching this holding, the court specifically noted that plaintiffs had failed to "detail any history of prosecution of state employees for participation in state medical marijuana licensing schemes."[111]

What Obligation, If Any, Does the U.S. Department of Justice Have to Enforce the Federal Prohibition on Marijuana?

Although the production, possession, or distribution of marijuana is a crime under federal law, DOJ has broad discretion in deciding whether to prosecute specific violations of the law. As previously discussed, DOJ has announced a policy that federal prosecutors "should not focus federal resources [] on individuals whose actions are in clear and unambiguous compliance with existing state laws providing for the medical use of marijuana."[112] Although recognizing that the conduct remains a violation of federal law, DOJ appears to have made a decision that prosecuting individual patients who are using marijuana for medicinal purposes is not an agency priority.

The established doctrine of "prosecutorial discretion" provides the federal government with "broad discretion" as to when, whom, and whether to prosecute for violations of federal law.[113] In granting this discretion, the courts have recognized that the "decision to prosecute is particularly ill-suited to judicial review," as it involves the consideration of factors—such as the strength of evidence, deterrence value, and existing enforcement priorities— "not readily susceptible to the kind of analysis the courts are competent to undertake."[114] Although prosecutorial discretion is subject to very few limitations, it is not "unfettered." For example, the selection of whom to prosecute is subject to the non-discrimination restrictions of the Equal Protection Clause.[115] Accordingly, prosecutors cannot base a decision to prosecute on "an unjustifiable standard such as race, religion, or other arbitrary classification."[116]

A decision by an individual prosecutor not to bring charges against an individual for violating the CSA's prohibition on the production, possession, or distribution of marijuana—assuming that decision is not grounded in a discriminatory purpose—would clearly fall within the umbrella of "prosecutorial discretion." Thus, there would appear to be no constitutional defect in a prosecutor's decision not to investigate or prosecute individuals who use marijuana for medicinal purposes in compliance with state law. DOJ has no obligation to prosecute all violations of federal law.[117]

Given DOJ's position, questions may be raised as to the extent to which DOJ may decline to enforce a duly enacted federal statute. For example, a formal decision to never prosecute specific conduct that Congress has expressly disallowed may raise constitutional concerns under the separation of powers.[118] However, DOJ's position, as established in the Ogden

Memorandum, does not appear to rise to such a repudiation of existing laws—either in its form or its scope. Rather, the decision to limit prosecutions appears to be based on enforcement priorities and the allocation of resources. Indeed, the Ogden Memorandum, in conjunction with the later Cole Memorandum, specifically states that the DOJ will continue to prosecute certain violations and, in fact, has done so.

CONCLUSION

The legal status of state laws respecting the use of medical marijuana remains ambiguous. Although state laws that merely exempt qualified users of medical marijuana from state prosecution have consistently survived preemption challenges, state laws that affirmatively authorize and regulate medical marijuana may pose a more serious "obstacle" to the accomplishment of federal objectives. Notwithstanding the many unresolved questions of preemption, this interplay between state and federal law has prompted a unique legal result. While an individual may be able to possess, distribute, or cultivate marijuana for limited purposes under state law, that same conduct remains a criminal offense under federal law. For example, operators of licensed marijuana dispensaries—which may represent legitimate licensed business ventures under state law—are subject to felony prosecutions under federal law at any time. Thus, it appears that it is generally the discretionary restraint of the federal government, in addition to the necessity to prioritize limited resources, that brings some modicum of stability to the interplay between state medical marijuana laws and the federal prohibition on the production, possession, and distribution of marijuana.

End Notes

[1] Controlled Substances Act, 21 U.S.C. §§801 et seq.
[2] 21 U.S.C. §812(b)(1).
[3] Theses states include Alaska, Arizona, California, Colorado, Delaware, Hawaii, Maine, Michigan, Montana, Nevada, New Jersey, New Mexico, Oregon, Rhode Island, Vermont, and Washington. In addition, the state of Maryland has a medical marijuana law that permits individuals arrested for possession of one ounce of marijuana or less to raise medical use as an affirmative defense at trial. Md. Ann. Code §5-601.
[4] U.S. Const., Art. VI, cl. 2 ("The Constitution, and the Laws of the United States which shall be made in Pursuance thereof; and all Treaties made, or which shall be made, under the Authority of the United States, shall be the supreme Law of the Land.").

[5] Memorandum for selected U.S. Attorneys from David W. Ogden, Deputy Attorney General, *Investigations and Prosecutions in States Authorizing the Medical Use of Marijuana*, October 19, 2009 (hereinafter Ogden Memorandum) *available at* http://www.justice.gov/opa/documents/medical-marijuana.pdf.

[6] *Id.*

[7] 21 U.S.C. §812. It should also be noted that the United States has treaty obligations to maintain effective controls over marijuana. *See, e.g.*, Single Convention on Narcotics Drugs, March 30, 1961, 18 U.S.T. 1409.

[8] 21 U.S.C. §§811-812.

[9] 21 U.S.C. §823.

[10] *See* 21 C.F.R. §1304.11(a) ("Each inventory shall contain a complete and accurate record of all controlled substances on hand ..."); *see also* 21 C.F.R. §1301.74(a) ("All applicants and registrants shall provide effective controls to guard against theft and diversion of controlled substances ...").

[11] 21 U.S.C. §812(b)(1).

[12] Very narrow exceptions to the federal prohibition do exist. For example, one may legally use marijuana if participating in an FDA approved study or participate in the Compassionate Investigational New Drug program.

[13] 21 U.S.C. §844(a).

[14] 21 U.S.C. §841(b).

[15] Ogden Memorandum, *supra* note 5.

[16] *Id.* at 1-2.

[17] *Id.* at 3.

[18] Memorandum for U.S. Attorneys from James M. Cole, Deputy Attorney General, *Guidance Regarding the Ogden Memo in Jurisdictions Seeking to Authorize Marijuana for Medical Use*, October 19, 2009 (hereinafter Cole Memorandum).

[19] *Id.* at 2.

[20] William Yardley, *New Federal Crackdown Confounds States that Allow Medical Marijuana*, N.Y. Times (May 7, 2011).

[21] *See*, Chad Livengood and Doug Denison, *Medical Marijuana Law Busted*, The News Journal (Delaware), February12, 2012; Olivia Katrandjian, *Under Federal Threat, Washington Governor Vetoes Medical Marijuana Dispensary Bill*, ABC News, April 30, 2011.

[22] Some states and localities, however, treat the possession of small amounts of marijuana (typically one ounce or less)as a civil, rather than criminal, offense. *See, e.g.*, Colo. Rev. Stat. §18-18-406 ("any person who possesses two ounces or less of marijuana commits a class 2 petty offense ... punished by a fine of not more than one hundred dollars.").

[23] State exemptions often apply not only to the patients, but also primary caregivers and physicians. *See, e.g.*, Nev. Rev. Stat. §453A.220.

[24] For purposes of this report, the term "state" includes the District of Columbia.

[25] *See, e.g.*, R.I. Gen Laws §21-28.6-4.

[26] California permits an "oral recommendation." Cal. Health & Safety Code §11362.5.

[27] *See, e.g.*, Wash. Rev. Code §69.51A.040.

[28] *See, e.g.*, Colo. Const. Art. XVIII §14.

[29] *See. e.g.*, Ore. Rev. Stat. §§475.316, 475.319.

[30] *See, e.g.*, Ariz. Rev. Stat. §36-2806.02.

[31] Cal. Health & Safety Code §11362.765.

[32] *See*, Robert A. Mikos, *On the Limits of Supremacy: Medical Marijuana and the States' Overlooked Power to Legalize Federal Crime*, 62 Vand. L. Rev. 1421, 1432 (2009) ("Most states, however have simply refused or neglected to address the issue ... This means that qualified patients must often resort to the black market to obtain the marijuana they are legally entitled to possess.").

[33] 545 U.S. 1 (2005).

[34] *Id.* at 15.

[35] *Id.* at 17-18 ("The similarities between this case and *Wickard* are striking."). In Wickard v. Filburn, 317 U.S. 111 (1942), the Court held that the Agricultural Adjustment Act's federal quota system applied to bushels of wheat that were homegrown and personally consumed.

[36] *Raich*, 545 U.S. at 19.

[37] *Id.* ("[T]he diversion of homegrown marijuana tends to frustrate the federal interest in eliminating commercial transactions in the interstate market in their entirety.").

[38] *Id.* at 22.

[39] *Id.* at 29.

[40] U.S. Const. amend. X ("The powers not delegated to the United States by the Constitution, nor prohibited by it to the States, are reserved to the States respectively, or to the people.").

[41] National League of Cities v. Usery, 426 U.S. 833 (1976).

[42] New York v. United States, 505 U.S. 144 (1992).

[43] *Id.*

[44] *Id.* at 175.

[45] 521 U.S. 898 (1997).

[46] *Id.* at 904-918.

[47] In *Reno v. Condon*, the Supreme Court held that a federal law does not "commandeer" state resources so long as it "does not require the States in their sovereign capacities to regulate their own citizens," but rather regulates state activities directly. 528 U.S. 141, 151 (2000).

[48] *See*, South Dakota v. Dole, 483 U.S. 203 (1987); *New York*, 505 U.S. at 188 (pointing out that the Spending Clause provides an alternative to the congressional "commandeering" of state officials that violated the Tenth Amendment).

[49] See, Printz v. United States, 521 U.S. 898, 933, 138 L. Ed. 2d 914, 117 S. Ct. 2365 (1997) (O'Connor, J., concurring) (discussing ability of state officials to voluntarily continue to participate in a federal program).

[50] *See, e.g.*, Wickard v. Filburn, 317 U.S. 111, 124 (1942)("[N]o form of state activity can constitutionally thwart the regulatory power granted by the commerce clause to Congress").

[51] 21 U.S.C. §903 (limiting the preemptive scope of the CSA to only those state laws that create a "positive conflict" with federal law).

[52] U.S. Const., Art. VI, cl. 2.

[53] Northern States Power Co. v. Minnesota, 447 F.2d 1143, 1145 (8th Cir. 1971).

[54] Rice v. Santa Fe Elevator Corp., 331 U.S. 218, 230 (1947).

[55] Hines v. Davidowitz, 312 U.S. 52, 67 (1941); *See also*, English v. General Elec. Co., 496 U.S. 72, 79 (1990) ("By referring to these three categories, we should not be taken to mean that they are rigidly distinct.").

[56] Skull Valley Band of Goshute Indians v. Nielson, 376 F.3d 1223, 1240 (10th Cir. 2004) (citing Wardair Canada, Inc. v. Florida Dep't of Revenue 477 U.S. 1 (1986)).

[57] *See, e.g.*, Norfolk & Western Ry. v. American Train Dispatchers' Ass'n, 499 U.S. 117 (1991).

[58] However, where Congress legislates in an area displacing "the historic police powers of the States," courts should imply preemption only where it is the "clear and manifest purpose of Congress." Rice v. Santa Fe Elevator Corp., 331 U.S. 218, 230 (1947).

[59] *See*, Gade v. National Solid Waste Management Assn., 505 U.S. 88, 98 (1992).

[60] *Santa Fe Elevator Corp.*, 331 U.S. at 230 (1947).

[61] 21 U.S.C. §903 (emphasis added).

[62] *Id.*

[63] *See, e.g.*, Emerald Steel Fabricators, Inc., v. Bureau of Labor and Industries, 348 Ore. 159 (2010); *But see*, County of San Diego v. San Diego Norml, 165 Cal. App. 4th 798 (2008)(holding that a state law conflicts with the CSA only where it is impossible to comply with both the state and federal law.).

[64] *See*, Wyeth v. Levine, 555 U.S. 555 (2009); Barnett Bank v. Nelson, 517 U.S. 25 (1996).

[65] *Barnett Bank*, 517 U.S. at 31. (holding that a federal statute that permitted national banks to sell insurance and a state statute that prohibited banks from selling insurance did not "impose directly conflicting duties").

[66] Freightliner Corp. v. Myrick, 514 U.S. 280, 287 (1947).

[67] Crosby v. National Foreign Trade Council, 530 U.S. 363, 373 (2000)(In considering obstacle preemption, a court's judgment is to be informed by "examining the federal statute as a whole and identifying its purpose and intended effects.").

[68] Id.

[69] Rice v. Santa Fe Elevator Corp., 331 U.S. 218 (1947).

[70] County of San Diego v. San Diego Norml, 165 Cal. App. 4th 798 (2008) (citing Boyle v. United Technologies Corp., 487 U.S. 500, 507 (1988)).

[71] See, e.g., United States v. Oakland Cannabis Buyers' Cooperative, 532 U.S. 483 (2001) (holding that there is no medical necessity defense under the CSA, even where state law recognizes such a defense.) United States v. Stacy, 734 F. Supp. 2d 1074 (S.D. Cal. 2010); United States v. Lynch, 2010 U.S. Dist. LEXIS 53011(C.D. Cal. 2010).

[72] Stacy, 734 F. Supp. at 1079 ("[T]he fact that an individual may not be prosecuted under [state] law does not provide him or her with immunity under federal law."); United states v. Rosenthal, 454 F.3d 943 (9th Cir. 2006) (holding that state medical marijuana law could not act as a shield to federal prosecution.)

[73] Stacy, 734 F. Supp. at 1084.

[74] See, Crosby, 530 U.S. at 373.

[75] Qualified Patients Assoc. v. City of Anaheim, 187 Cal. App. 4th 734 (2010) (citing Conant v. Walters, 309 F.3d 629, 646 (9th Cir. 2002) (Kozinski, J. concurring) ("That patients may be more likely to violate federal law if the additional deterrent of state liability is removed may worry the federal government, but the proper response—according to New York and Printz—is to ratchet up the federal regulatory regime, not to commandeer that of the state.").

[76] Cal. Health & Safety Code §11362.5.

[77] Id.

[78] People v. Kelly, 222 P.3d 186 (Cal. 2010).

[79] Cal. Health & Safety Code §11362.765.

[80] See, Assenberg, et al. v. Anacortes Housing Authority, 2006 U.S. Dist. LEXIS 34002 (W.D. Wash. 2006)("[T]o the extent that the state law legalizes marijuana use and prohibits the forfeiture of public housing, it conflicts with the CSAand the federal statutes and regulations that criminalize marijuana use and prohibit illegal drug use in public housing.").

[81] Mikos, supra note 32 at 1457-59 ("A handful of states have proposed supplying marijuana directly to qualified patients via state-operated farms and distribution centers ... The CSA, however, clearly preempts any such state program.). Professor Mikos notes that both Maine and New Mexico have "seriously considered supplying marijuana directly to qualified patients through state-run distribution centers." Id. at 1432.

[82] State courts in states with medical marijuana laws have been at the forefront of marijuana preemption litigation. Some of these cases arise as a result of localities challenging state medical marijuana laws—and the obligations those laws place on the localities—as preempted under the CSA. See, e.g., City of Riverside v. Inland Empire Patient's Health and Wellness Center, Inc., 200 Cal. App. 4th 885 (2011), review granted, 2012 Cal. LEXIS 1028 (Cal. January 18, 2012).

[83] Cal. Health & Safety Code §11362.71; Ore. Rev. Stat. §475.306.

[84] 165 Cal. App. 4th 798 (2008), review denied 2008 Cal. LEXIS 12220 (Cal. 2008).

[85] Id. at 808-809.

[86] Id. at 819 ("Congress intended to reject express and field preemption of state laws concerning controlled substances.").

[87] Id. at 823.

[88] Id. at 826-28.

[89] Id. at 825.

[90] Id. at 827. In what may be interpreted as a limiting paragraph, the court also noted that "[a]lthough California's decision to enact statutory exemptions from state criminal

prosecution for such persons arguably undermines the goals or is inconsistent with the CSA—a question we do not decide here—any alleged 'obstacle' to the federal goals is presented by those California statutes that create the exemptions, not by the statutes providing a system for rapidly identifying exempt individuals.").

[91] 348 Ore. 159 (2010).

[92] *Id.* at 525.

[93] *Id.* at 520-22.

[94] O.R.S. §659A.112.

[95] *Emerald Steel*, 348 Ore. at 521.

[96] *Id.* at 526.

[97] *Id.* at 527-28.

[98] *Id.* at 528 ("To be sure, the two laws are logically inconsistent; state law authorizes what federal law prohibits. However, a person can comply with both laws by refraining from any use of marijuana ...").

[99] *Id.* at 529.

[100] *Id.* at 530 ("[T]he validity of the exemptions and the validity of the authorization turn on different constitutional principles.").

[101] *Id.*

[102] Additionally, how important is the fact that *Emerald Steel* arose in an employment discrimination dispute? Would the Court have reached the same conclusion if the case arose in a different context?

[103] *See, e.g.*, 21 U.S.C. §846 (making it illegal to conspire to violate the CSA); 18 U.S.C. §§2-4, 371.

[104] *See, e.g.*, Ore. Rev. Stat. §475.323.

[105] 21 U.S.C. §885(d).

[106] *See*, State v. Karma, 39 P.3d 866 (Or. App. 2002)(finding immunity for city police). If a state officer is acting pursuant to a preempted state medical marijuana provision, it is an open question as to whether he be "lawfully engaged in the enforcement of any law ..."

[107] Letter from Jenny A. Durkan, U.S. Attorney for the Western District of Washington and Michael C. Ormsby, U.S. Attorney for the Eastern District of Washington, to the Honorable Christine Gregoire, Washington State Governor, April 14, 2011. 108 *Id.*

[109] Arizona v. United States, Case No. CV 11-1072-PHX-SRB (D.C. Ariz. January 4, 2012) at 3. Governors of five other states have reportedly received similar letters. William Yardley, *New Federal Crackdown Confounds States that Allow Medical Marijuana*, N.Y. Times (May 7, 2011).

[110] Arizona v. United States, Case No. CV 11-1072-PHX-SRB (D.C. Ariz. January 4, 2012) at 7.

[111] *Id.* at 8.

[112] Ogden Memorandum, *supra* note 5 at 1-2.

[113] United States v. Goodwin, 457 U.S. 368, 380 (1982).

[114] Wayte v. United States, 470 U.S. 598, 607 (1985).

[115] United States v. Batchelder, 442 U.S. 114, 125 (1979).

[116] Oyler v. Boles, 368 U.S. 448, 456 (1962).

[117] *Batchelder*, 442 U.S. at 124 ("Whether to prosecute ... [is a] decision[] that generally rest[s] in the prosecutor's discretion.").

[118] The President has the constitutional obligation to "take care that the laws be faithfully executed." U.S. Const. Art II, §3. Moreover, although the effect of the provision is debated, 28 U.S.C. §547 directs that "except as otherwise provided by law, each United States attorney, within his district, shall—prosecute for all offenses against the United States ..."

In: The Medical Marijuana Question ...   ISBN: 978-1-62417-080-5
Editors: C. Gable and M. Feuerstein   © 2013 Nova Science Publishers, Inc.

Chapter 2

THE DEA POSITION ON MARIJUANA*

U.S. Department of Justice

Marijuana is properly categorized under Schedule I of the Controlled Substances Act (CSA), 21 U.S.C. § 801, et seq. The clear weight of the currently available evidence supports this classification, including evidence that smoked marijuana has a high potential for abuse, has no accepted medicinal value in treatment in the United States, and evidence that there is a general lack of accepted safety for its use even under medical supervision.

The campaign to legitimize what is called "medical" marijuana is based on two propositions: first, that science views marijuana as medicine; and second, that the DEA targets sick and dying people using the drug. Neither proposition is true. Specifically, smoked marijuana has not withstood the rigors of science–it is not medicine, and it is not safe. Moreover, the DEA targets criminals engaged in the cultivation and trafficking of marijuana, not the sick and dying. This is true even in the 15 states that have approved the use of "medical" marijuana.[1]

On October 19, 2009 Attorney General Eric Holder announced formal guidelines for federal prosecutors in states that have enacted laws authorizing the use of marijuana for medical purposes. The guidelines, as set forth in a memorandum from Deputy Attorney General David W. Ogden, makes clear

---

* This is an edited, reformatted and augmented version of the Drug Enforcement Agency, dated January 2011.

that the focus of federal resources should not be on individuals whose actions are in compliance with existing state laws, and underscores that the Department will continue to prosecute people whose claims of compliance with state and local law conceal operations inconsistent with the terms, conditions, or purposes of the law. He also reiterated that the Department of Justice is committed to the enforcement of the Controlled Substances Act in all states and that this guidance does not "legalize" marijuana or provide for legal defense to a violation of federal law.[2] While some people have interpreted these guidelines to mean that the federal government has relaxed its policy on "medical" marijuana, this in fact is not the case. Investigations and prosecutions of violations of state and federal law will continue. These are the guidelines DEA has and will continue to follow.

THE FALLACY OF MARIJUANA FOR MEDICINAL USE

Smoked Marijuana Is Not Medicine

In 1970, Congress enacted laws against marijuana based in part on its conclusion that marijuana has no scientifically proven medical value. Likewise, the Food and Drug Administration (FDA), which is responsible for approving drugs as safe and effective medicine, has thus far declined to approve smoked marijuana for any condition or disease. Indeed, the FDA has noted that "there is currently sound evidence that smoked marijuana is harmful," and "that no sound scientific studies support medical use of marijuana for treatment in the United States, and no animal or human data support the safety or efficacy of marijuana for general medical use."[3]

The United States Supreme Court has also declined to carve out an exception for marijuana under a theory of medical viability. In 2001, for example, the Supreme Court decided that a 'medical necessity' defense against prosecution was unavailable to defendants because Congress had purposely placed marijuana into Schedule I, which enumerates those controlled substances without any medical benefits. *See United States v. Oakland Cannabis Buyers' Cooperative et al.*, 532 U.S. 483, 491-92 (2001).

In *Gonzales v. Raich*, 545 U.S. 1 (2005), the Court had another opportunity to create a type of 'medical necessity' defense in a case involving severely ill California residents who had received physician approval to cultivate and use marijuana under California's Compassionate Use Act (CUA). *See Raich*, 545 U.S. at 9. Despite the state's attempt to shield its residents from liability under CUA, the Supreme Court held that Congress' power to regulate interstate drug markets included the authority to regulate wholly intrastate markets as well. Consequently, the Court again declined to carve out a 'medical necessity' defense, finding that the CSA was not diminished in the face of any state law to the contrary and could support the specific enforcement actions at issue.

In a show of support for the *Raich* decision, the International Narcotics Control Board (INCB) issued this statement urging other countries to consider the real dangers of cannabis:

> Cannabis is classified under international conventions as a drug with a number of personal and public health problems. It is not a 'soft' drug as some people would have you believe. There is new evidence confirming well-known mental health problems, and some countries with a more liberal policy towards cannabis are reviewing their position. Countries need to take a strong stance towards cannabis abuse.[4]

The DEA and the federal government are not alone in viewing smoked marijuana as having no documented medical value. Voices in the medical community likewise do not accept smoked marijuana as medicine:

- The **American Medical Association (AMA)** has always endorsed "well-controlled studies of marijuana and related cannabinoids in patients with serious conditions for which preclinical, anecdotal, or controlled evidence suggests possible efficacy and the application of such results to the understanding and treatment of disease." In November 2009, the AMA amended its policy, urging that marijuana's status as a Schedule I controlled substance be reviewed "with the goal of facilitating the conduct of clinical research and development of cannabinoid-based medicines, and alternate delivery methods." The AMA also stated that "this should not be viewed as an endorsement of state-based medical cannabis programs, the legalization of marijuana, or that scientific evidence on the therapeutic use of cannabis meets the current standards for prescription drug product."[5]
- The **American Society of Addiction Medicine's (ASAM)** public policy statement on "Medical Marijuana," clearly rejects smoking as a means of drug delivery. ASAM further recommends that "all cannabis, cannabis-based products and cannabis delivery devices should be subject to the same standards applicable to all other

prescription medication and medical devices, and should not be distributed or otherwise provided to patients ..." without FDA approval. ASAM also "discourages state interference in the federal medication approval process."[6]

- The **American Cancer Society (ACS)** "does not advocate inhaling smoke, nor the legalization of marijuana," although the organization does support carefully controlled clinical studies for alternative delivery methods, specifically a tetrahydrocannabinol (THC) skin patch.[7]

- The **American Glaucoma Society (AGS)** has stated that "although marijuana can lower the intraocular pressure, the side effects and short duration of action, coupled with the lack of evidence that its use alters the course of glaucoma, preclude recommending this drug in any form for the treatment of glaucoma at the present time."[8]

- The **American Academy of Pediatrics (AAP)** believes that "[a]ny change in the legal status of marijuana, even if limited to adults, could affect the prevalence of use among adolescents." While it supports scientific research on the possible medical use of cannabinoids as opposed to smoked marijuana, it opposes the legalization of marijuana.[9]

- The **National Multiple Sclerosis Society (NMSS)** has stated that it could not recommend medical marijuana be made widely available for people with multiple sclerosis for symptom management, explaining: "This decision was not only based on existing legal barriers to its use but, even more importantly, because studies to date do not demonstrate a clear benefit compared to existing symptomatic therapies and because side effects, systemic effects, and long-term effects are not yet clear."[10]

- The **British Medical Association (BMA)** voiced extreme concern that downgrading the criminal status of marijuana would "mislead" the public into believing that the drug is safe. The BMA maintains that marijuana "has been linked to greater risk of heart disease, lung cancer, bronchitis and emphysema."[11] The 2004 Deputy Chairman of the BMA's Board of Science said that "[t]he public must be made aware of the harmful effects we know result from smoking this drug."[12]

In 1999, **The Institute of Medicine (IOM)** released a landmark study reviewing the supposed medical properties of marijuana. The study is frequently cited by "medical" marijuana advocates, but in fact severely undermines their arguments.

- After release of the IOM study, the principal investigators cautioned that the active compounds in marijuana may have medicinal potential and therefore should be researched further. However, the study concluded that "there is little future in smoked marijuana as a medically approved medication."[13]
- For some ailments, the IOM found "...potential therapeutic value of cannabinoid drugs, primarily THC, for pain relief, control of nausea and vomiting, and appetite stimulation."[14] However, it pointed out that "[t]he effects of cannabinoids on the symptoms studied are generally modest, and in most cases there are more effective medications [than smoked marijuana]."[15]
- The study concluded that, at best, there is only anecdotal information on the medical benefits of smoked marijuana for some ailments, such as muscle spasticity. For other ailments, such as epilepsy and glaucoma, the study found no evidence of medical value and did not endorse further research.[16]
- The IOM study explained that "smoked marijuana . . . is a crude THC delivery system that also delivers harmful substances." In addition, "plants contain a variable mixture of biologically active compounds and cannot be expected to provide a precisely defined drug effect." Therefore, the study concluded that "there is little future in smoked marijuana as a medically approved medication."[17]
- The principal investigators explicitly stated that using smoked marijuana in clinical trials "should not be designed to develop it as a licensed drug, but should be a stepping stone to the development of new, safe delivery systems of cannabinoids."[18]

Thus, even scientists and researchers who believe that certain active ingredients in marijuana may have potential medicinal value openly *discount the notion that smoked marijuana is or can become "medicine."*

The Drug Enforcement Administration supports ongoing research into potential medicinal uses of marijuana's active ingredients. As of December 2010:

- There are 111 researchers registered with DEA to perform studies with marijuana, marijuana extracts, and non-tetrahydrocannabinol marijuana derivatives that exist in the plant, such as cannabidiol and cannabinol.
- Studies include evaluation of abuse potential, physical/psychological effects, adverse effects, therapeutic potential, and detection.
- Fourteen of the researchers are approved to conduct research with smoked marijuana on human subjects.[19]

At present, however, *the clear weight of the evidence is that smoked marijuana is harmful.* No matter what medical condition has been studied, other drugs already approved by the FDA have been proven to be safer than smoked marijuana.

The only drug currently approved by the FDA that contains the synthetic form of THC is Marinol®. Available through prescription, Marinol® comes in pill form, and is used to relieve nausea and vomiting associated with chemotherapy for cancer patients and to assist with loss of appetite with AIDS patients.

Sativex®, an oromucosal spray for the treatment of spasticity due to Multiple Sclerosis is already approved for use in Canada and was approved in June 2010 for use in the United Kingdom. The oral liquid spray contains two of the cannabinoids found in marijuana – THC and cannabidiol (CBD) -but unlike smoked marijuana, removes contaminants, reduces the intoxicating effects, is grown in a structured and scientific environment, administers a set dosage and meets criteria for pharmaceutical products.[20]

The legalization movement is not simply a harmless academic exercise. The mortal danger of thinking that marijuana is "medicine" was graphically illustrated by a story from California. In the spring of 2004, Irma Perez was "in the throes of her first experience with the drug Ecstasy... when, after taking one Ecstasy tablet, she became ill and told friends that she felt like she was...'going to die'... Two teenage acquaintances did not seek medical care and instead tried to get Perez to smoke marijuana. When that failed due to her seizures, the friends tried to force-feed marijuana leaves to her, "apparently because [they] knew that drug is sometimes used to treat cancer patients." Irma Perez lost consciousness and died a few days later when she was taken off life support. She was 14 years old.[21]

Organizers behind the "medical" marijuana movement have not dealt with ensuring that the product meets the standards of modern medicine: quality, safety and efficacy. There is no standardized composition or dosage; no appropriate prescribing information; no quality control; no accountability for the product; no safety regulation; no way to measure its effectiveness (besides anecdotal stories); and no insurance coverage. Science, not popular vote, should determine what medicine is.

The Legalization Lobby

The proposition that smoked marijuana is "medicine" is, in sum, false—trickery used by those promoting wholesale legalization.

- The Marijuana Policy Project (MPP) provides funding and assistance to states and localities to promote "marijuana as medicine" initiatives and legislation. Yet their vision statement clearly indicates that they have a much broader goal of decriminalizing marijuana. At the same time the marijuana legalization proponents are soliciting support for laws allowing marijuana to be used as medicine, they are working to *modify policies to regulate marijuana similarly to alcohol.*[22]
- Ed Rosenthal, senior editor of *High Times*, a pro-drug magazine, once revealed the legalization strategy behind the "medical" marijuana movement. While addressing an effort to seek public sympathy for glaucoma patients, he said, "I have to tell you that I also use marijuana medically. I have a latent glaucoma which has never been diagnosed. The reason why it's never been diagnosed is because I've been treating it." He continued, "I have to be honest, there is another reason why I do use marijuana . . . and that is because I like to get high. Marijuana is fun."[23]
- A few billionaires—not broad grassroots support—started and sustain the "medical" marijuana and drug legalization movements in the United States. Without their money and influence, the drug legalization movement would shrivel. According to National Families in Action, four individuals—George Soros, Peter Lewis, George Zimmer, and John Sperling—contributed $1,510,000 to the effort to pass a "medical" marijuana law in California in 1996, a sum representing nearly 60 percent of the total contributions.[24]

- In 2000, *The New York Times* interviewed Ethan Nadelmann, Director of the Lindesmith Center. Responding to criticism that the medical marijuana issue is a stalking horse for drug legalization, Mr. Nadelmann stated: "Will it help lead toward marijuana legalization? . . . I hope so."[25]

- When a statute dramatically reducing penalties for "medical" marijuana took effect in Maryland in October 2003, a defense attorney noted that "[t]here are a whole bunch of people who like marijuana who can now try to use this defense." The attorney observed that lawyers would be "neglecting their clients if they did not try to find out what 'physical, emotional or psychological'" condition could be enlisted to develop a defense to justify a defendant's using the drug. "Sometimes people are self-medicating without even realizing it," he said.[26]

- In 2004, Alaska voters faced a ballot initiative that would have made it legal for adults age 21 and older to possess, grow, buy, or give away marijuana. The measure also called for state regulation and taxation of the drug. The campaign was funded almost entirely by the Washington, D.C.-based MPP, which provided "almost all" the $857,000 taken in by the pro-marijuana campaign. Fortunately, Alaskan voters rejected the initiative.[27]

- In October 2005, Denver voters passed Initiative 100 decriminalizing marijuana based on incomplete and misleading campaign advertisements put forth by the Safer Alternative for Enjoyable Recreation (SAFER). A Denver City Councilman complained that the group used the slogan "Make Denver SAFER" on billboards and campaign signs to mislead the voters into thinking that the initiative supported increased police staffing. Indeed, the Denver voters were never informed of the initiative's true intent to decriminalize marijuana.[28]

- In 2006, the legalization movement funded three state marijuana-related initiatives, which were defeated in the November election. In Colorado, SAFER was behind Amendment 44, which allowed for possession of up to one ounce of marijuana. The amendment was defeated by 60 percent of the vote. In Nevada, Question 7, which was supported by the MPP, sought to permit the manufacture, distribution, and sale of marijuana to adults aged 21 or older. The measure was defeated by 56 percent of the vote. In South Dakota, South Dakotans for Medical Marijuana pushed Measure 4, allowing medical marijuana access. The measure was defeated by 52 percent of the vote.[29]

- The legalization movement was more successful at the local level in 2006. MPP-funded local groups were able to pass measures in three California cities: Santa Barbara (Sensible Santa Barbara), Santa Cruz (Santa Cruz Citizens for Sensible Marijuana Policy), and Santa Monica (Santa Monicans for Sensible Marijuana Policy); and in Missoula, Montana (Citizens for Responsible Crime Policy). Residents voted to make marijuana possession the lowest law enforcement priority in their cities.[30]

- Three other legalization groups also won local initiatives: the NORML (the National Organization for the Reform of Marijuana Laws) chapter at the University of Arkansas at Fayetteville helped make possession of one ounce or less of marijuana a misdemeanor in Eureka Springs, Arkansas; Americans for Safe Access assisted Albany, CA with passing Measure D, allowing a medical marijuana dispensary in the City of Albany; and the Drug Policy Forum of Massachusetts helped four districts pass non-binding policy statements from voters allowing for possession of up to one ounce of marijuana be a civil violation subject only to a $100 fine (2 districts) and allowing seriously ill patients to possess and grow marijuana with a doctor's recommendation.[31]

- In 2007 in Hailey, Idaho, the ballot initiatives to legalize industrial hemp, legalize medical use of marijuana and to allow marijuana laws to receive the lowest enforcement priority passed, but have not been implemented. The initiative to regulate and tax marijuana sales and use failed. Mayor Rick Davis, City Councilman Don Keirn, and Chief of Police Jeff Gunter filed a Declaratory Judgment action alleging that the three initiatives were illegal. "The lawsuit primarily alleges that the three initiatives are illegal because they are contrary to the general laws of the State of Idaho and the United States."[32] Ryan Davidson, director of The Liberty Lobby of Idaho, put the initiatives back on the May ballot, and again they passed. "Davidson's efforts in Hailey are part of a larger grassroots agenda to have marijuana laws reformed statewide and nationally."[33] In March, 2009 Blaine County 5th District Court Judge Robert Elgee filed a decision to void the initiatives that would have legalized marijuana use in the city and would have made enforcement of marijuana laws the lowest priority for Hailey police.

The judge also voided language in the initiative that would have required individual city officials to advocate for marijuana reform.[34]

- In 2008, with support from the Michigan Coalition for Compassionate Care, Michigan became the 13th state to approve marijuana for medicinal purposes.[35]
- Massachusetts, backed by the Committee for Sensible Marijuana Policy, replaced criminal penalties for one ounce of marijuana with a civil fine in 2008.[36]
- Voters in four districts (15 towns) in Massachusetts, supported by local legalization groups, passed a ballot measure to instruct a representative from each district to vote in favor of legislation that would allow seriously ill patients, with a doctor's written recommendation, to possess and grow small amounts of marijuana for their personal medical use.[37]
- In the same year, voters in Fayetteville, Arkansas, supported by Sensible Fayetteville, voted to make adult marijuana possession law the lowest priority for local law enforcement.[38]
- In California, Proposition 5, also known as the Non-Violent Offender Rehabilitation Act, and supported by the Drug Policy Alliance, called for more funding for addiction treatment and decriminalization of up to an ounce of marijuana. This initiative did not pass.[39]
- The legalizers were also less successful in New Hampshire, where although the state legislature approved a bill to legalize "medical" marijuana, Governor John Lynch vetoed the bill in July 2009, citing concerns over cultivation, distribution and the potential for abuse.[40]
- Rhode Island became the 3rd state to allow the sale of marijuana for medicinal purposes. In June 2009, the Rhode Island legislature overrode Governor Circieri's veto of bills that allow for the establishment of three compassionate care centers regulated by the state department of health.[41]
- New Mexico opened its first "medical" marijuana dispensary in June 2009, becoming the 4th state to allow "medical" marijuana dispensaries.[42]
- In November 2009, Maine became the 5th state to allow dispensaries. The voters also approved the expansion of the "medical" marijuana law, to include defining debilitating medical conditions and incorporating additional diseases that can be included under the law. This effort was funded by the Drug Policy Alliance.[43]

- On November 4, 2009, Breckenridge, Colorado citizens voted to decriminalize possession of up to 1 ounce of marijuana for adults over 21 years of age. The measure, however, is symbolic, because pot possession is still against state law. Sean McAllister, a Breckenridge lawyer who pushed for the decriminalization measure said that "the vote shows people want to skip medical marijuana and legalize pot for everyone."[44]

- In January 2010, New Jersey became the 14th state to allow the use of marijuana for medicinal purposes. With the most restrictive law in the country, only residents with one of twelve chronic illnesses (not including chronic pain) will be able to get a prescription from their doctor to buy up to two ounces a month from one of six dispensaries.[45] Implementation of the program, originally scheduled for October 1, 2010, has been extended by the state legislature until January 1, 2011, to give the Governor more time to determine who will grow and dispense marijuana.[46] As of January 31, 2011 final details of the program were still being negotiated.

- In Massachusetts voters in 18 legislative districts approved non-binding measures calling on state lawmakers to pass 'medical' marijuana legislation or a bill to regulate marijuana like alcohol. The organizers of these measures included the Drug Policy Forum of Massachusetts, the Massachusetts Cannabis Reform Coalition, Suffolk University NORML and the University of Massachusetts Amherst Cannabis Reform Coalition.[47]

- In November 2010, Arizona became the 15th state to allow the use of marijuana for medicinal purposes. Proposition 203, the Arizona Medical Marijuana Act, sponsored by the Arizona Medical Marijuana Policy Project with financial support from George Soros, passed with 50.13 percent of the vote. The program, which will be established and implemented by the Department of Health Services, allows residents with certain medical conditions to obtain a doctor's written certification to purchase up to 2.5 ounces of marijuana every two weeks from a state approved dispensary or grow their own if they live 25 miles or more from a dispensary.[48]

- In South Dakota residents once again refused to support efforts to legalize marijuana. Measure 13, which sought to authorize the possession, use and cultivation of marijuana by and for persons with specific debilitating medical conditions, was defeated by 63.3 percent of the vote.[49]

- In Oregon 58 percent of the voters said no to Measure 74, which would have established a 'medical' marijuana supply system and allow for the sale of marijuana and marijuana-laced products in shops throughout the state. The measure was financially backed by billionaire Peter Lewis, a known legalization activist, who resides in Florida.[50]
- In California, voters defeated Proposition 19 (The Regulate, Control and Tax Cannabis Act of 2010), which sought to legalize the possession and cultivation of limited amounts of marijuana for use by individuals 21 years of age and older. Had it passed, California would have been the first state to legalize marijuana for recreational purposes.[51] The initiative garnered much debate. Fueled by financial support from legalization activists, including one million dollars each from Oakland cannabis entrepreneur Richard Lee and billionaire George Soros, proponents for the initiative used the media to attempt to sway public opinion.[52] Nine former DEA Administrators called upon U.S. Attorney General Eric H. Holder Jr. to clarify the federal position and reiterate the law.[53] In response, Attorney General Holder stated the Department of Justice's position.

"...the Department of Justice will remain firmly committed to enforcing the Controlled Substances Act (CSA) in all states. Prosecution of those who manufacture, distribute or possess any illegal drugs – including marijuana – and the disruption of drug trafficking organizations is a core priority of the Department. Accordingly, we will vigorously enforce the CSA against those individuals and organization who possess, manufacture, or distribute marijuana for recreational use, even if such activities are permitted under state law."[54]

- On July 25, 2007, the U.S. House of Representatives defeated, by a vote of 165-262, an amendment (HR-3093) that would have prevented the DEA and the Department of Justice from arresting or prosecuting medical marijuana patients and providers in the 12 states where medical marijuana was then legal. [55]
- Two Congressional initiatives on marijuana also failed in 2008. HR5842, Medical Marijuana Patient Protection Act and HR5843, Act to Remove Federal Penalties for the Personal Use of Marijuana by Responsible Adults, both died in committee.
- Three Congressional initiatives were introduced in Congress in 2009: HR2835 Medical Marijuana Patient Protection Act; HR2943 Personal

Use of Marijuana by Responsible Adults Act of 2009; and HR3939 Truth in Trials Act. None were passed.

- The Consolidated Appropriations Act of 2010 (HR 3288) became law in December 2009 without the "Barr Amendment," a provision that has been included in the Appropriations bill for the District of Columbia since 1999.[56] The Barr Amendment had prohibited "… any funds to be used to conduct a ballot initiative which seeks to legalize or reduce the penalties associated with the possession, use, or distribution of any Schedule I substance under the Controlled Substances Act (or any tetrahydrocannabinois derivative)."[57]

- The elimination of the Barr Amendment enabled the District of Columbia to implement Initiative 59, a ballot initiative that was approved in 1998 to allow for the use of marijuana for medical treatment. In May 2010, the District of Columbia City Council approved a bill that would allow chronically ill patients to receive a doctor's prescription to use marijuana and buy up to two ounces a month from a city-sanctioned distribution center. The Legalization of Marijuana for Medical Treatment Amendment Act of 2010 became law in July. The District of Columbia government is still working on the details of the program to ensure strict regulatory controls are in place prior to implementation.[58]

The Failure of Legalized Marijuana Efforts

The argument that "caregivers" who participate in legalized marijuana efforts are "compassionate" is contradicted by revelations that all too often cannabis clubs are fronts for drug dealers, not health facilities. Even the author of Proposition 215 believes the program is "a joke."

- Reverend Scott T. Imler, co-author of Proposition 215, the 1996 ballot initiative that legalized medical marijuana in California, expressed his disappointment with the way the program has been implemented in a series of interviews in late 2006.
  - "We created Prop. 215 so patients would not have to deal with black market profiteers. But today it is all about the money. Most of the dispensaries operating in California are a little more than dope dealers with store fronts."[59]

- "When we wrote 215, we were selling it to the public as something for seriously ill people....It's turned into a joke. I think a lot of people have medicalized their recreational use."[60]
- "What we set out to do was put something in the statutes that said medicine was a defense in case they got arrested using marijuana for medical reasons," Imler says. "What we got was a whole different thing, a big new industry."[61]
- In an interview with National Public Radio in August 2009, Reverend Imler stated that he believes that the law has been subverted. "What we have is de-facto legalization." The article continues, "He never envisioned that medicinal pot would turn into a business, open to virtually anyone."[62]

Rev. Imler's observations that 'its all about the money' are consistent with the financial realities that have been exposed by criminal investigations of cannabis clubs or dispensaries. Cannabis clubs or dispensaries are generating disproportionately large sums of cash through the sales of marijuana and marijuana tainted products when they should be operating as essentially nonprofit enterprises.

- Under California State law, financial responsibilities of cannabis clubs are governed, in part, by the Health & Safety § 11362.765 (c) and the California Attorney General's Guidelines for the Security and Non-diversion of Marijuana Grown for Medical Use Attorney (August 2008), which states in relevant part: "a primary caregiver who receives compensation for actual expenses, including reasonable compensation incurred for services provided to an eligible qualified patient or person with an identification card to enable that person to use marijuana under this article, or for payment for out-of-pocket expenses incurred in providing those services...."
- Both by statute and the Guidelines, revenue is framed in the context of "compensation for actual expenses" which should not be attributed beyond those "actual expenses" incurred through the manufacturing of marijuana by the primary caregiver, and only for those limited and quantified "patients."
- Further the statute, Guidelines and the courts have affirmed reasonable compensation for services or out-of-pocket expenses need to be confined to the context of the primary caregiver wherein those

services and out-of-pocket expenses relate to the housing, health, or safety of the qualified patient.

- Therefore, the acquisition of marijuana from the illicit open market and large scale commercial cultivation operations is beyond the statutory limited immunity and renders the commercial enterprise illicit by nature, whether or not resold at cost or at a loss.

Cannabis clubs or dispensaries are generating disproportionately large sums of cash through the sales of marijuana and marijuana tainted products when they should be operating as essentially nonprofit enterprises. Most of these profits are going unreported. According to the California Board of Equalization, the state collects anywhere from $58 million to $105 million in taxes from medical marijuana each year from approximately $700 million to $1.3 billion in marijuana sales.[63]

- "There is a clear indication that many dispensaries are intentionally evading their taxes, distributing illegal products and may be laundering illegally acquired money," Jerome E. Horton, California State Board of Equalization Vice Chairperson.[64]

Additionally, the Board of Equalization estimated in 2008 that about 300 dispensaries currently pay taxes, with another 500 evading them[65] (other media outlets have estimated the number of dispensaries to be between 1000-and 1500). If the tax and revenue projections are based on the 300 reporting entities, then, based on California Board of Equalization estimates, total medical marijuana revenues are between $1.87 and $3.47 billion per year.

It is a well proven maxim that the money from illegal drugs is so substantial that it attracts organized criminal groups and makes criminals out of otherwise honest citizens. All of this is proving true with the cannabis clubs.

- For example: On November 21, Luke Scarmazzo and Ricardo Montes were sentenced in the Eastern District of California to 262 months and 240 months imprisonment, respectively. A forfeiture judgment of $8.89 million was imposed. Scarmazzo and Montes were convicted on May 15 of engaging in a Continuing Criminal Enterprise, possession with intent to distribute marijuana, and firearms charges. From 2004 to 2006, Scarmazzo and Montes operated California Healthcare Collective, a medical marijuana dispensary, in Modesto, California, from where they sold marijuana to approximately 400 customers per day, exceeding $9 million in drug proceeds. This 34-month investigation resulted in the arrest of nine individuals, and the seizure of 1,000 marijuana plants, $330,000 in U.S. currency, and 11 firearms.[66]

- Drug proceeds generated by dispensaries taint more than just their owners. Depository institutions (banks, savings and loans, etc) that knowingly avail and continue to afford their products and services to commercialized cannabis cooperatives or clubs in order to meet payroll, utilities, security, maintain leases and acquire additional merchandise, do so in violation of federal anti-money laundering statutes by promoting the specified unlawful activity of drug trafficking.

In Oregon, where voters legalized "medical" marijuana for qualifying patients in November 1998, patients must grow their own marijuana or have a licensed grower provide it for them through an unpaid arrangement. While the initiative had good intentions, numerous problems exist.

- According to Lt. Michael Dingeman, Director of the Oregon State Police Drug Enforcement Section, many calls from cardholders are about never receiving the marijuana from their designated growers. The "growers are simply using the cardholders for cover, and selling their crops on the black market. In fact, some county sheriffs estimate that as much as one half of the illegal street marijuana they're seeing is being grown under the protection of the state's medical marijuana program."[67]
- Deputy Chief Tim George of the Medford Police Department says that the region is "swimming in weed," and the problem keeps getting worse. "People are traveling with large sums of money to buy marijuana. Weed is being shipped out of Oregon at record levels. Medical Marijuana has made it easier for criminals to grow it."[68]
- Sergeant Erik Fisher of the Drug Enforcement Section of the Oregon State Police says that the perception of the marijuana drug trade is mellower than other drug operations is wrong." He notes that almost all the distributors and growers carry firearms. "The other striking trend has been the increase in home invasion robberies of medical marijuana folks, and how absolutely violent they can be. We have more home invasions going on with medical marijuana people than any other drug dealer I can think of."[69]

Neighborhood residents, doctors and other professionals associated with marijuana dispensaries admit there have been problems.

- In a letter to the Editor of the Denver Post, Dr. Christian Thurstone, Medical Director of an Adolescent Substance Abuse Treatment Program in Denver, has seen what impact Colorado's policies regarding "medical" marijuana has had on young adults.
  - "About 95 percent of the hundreds of young people referred to my clinic each year have problems with marijuana. I see teenagers who choose pot over family, school, friends and health every day. When they're high, these young people make poor choices that lead to unplanned pregnancies, sexually transmitted diseases, school dropouts and car accidents that harm people. When teenagers are withdrawing from marijuana, they can be aggressive and get into fights or instigate conflicts that lead to more trouble."
  - Dr. Thurstone talks about a 19-year-old who he was treating for severe addiction for several months. "He recently showed up at my clinic with a medical marijuana license. How did he get it? He paid $300 for a brief visit with another doctor to discuss his "depression." The doctor took a cursory medical history that certainly didn't involve contacting me. The teenager walked out with the paperwork needed not only for a license to smoke it, but also for a license permitting a "caregiver" to grow up to six marijuana plants for him. My patient, who had quit using addictive substances after a near-death experience, is back to smoking marijuana daily, along with his caregiver."
  - In a three month period, Dr. Thurstone saw over a dozen patients between 18 and 25 with histories of substance abuse who had received a recommendation from other doctors to smoke marijuana.
  - "Kids without licenses tell me about potent pot they buy from caregivers whose plants yield enough supply to support sales on the side."[70]
- The White Mountain Independent reported that "In Colorado treatment centers, clinicians are treating more and more teens for marijuana addiction since the state legalized marijuana for medicinal use. At the Denver Health Medical Center, treatment for referrals has

tripled with 83 percent of teens that smoke pot daily saying that they obtained it from a medical marijuana patient."[71]

- A study by the Associated Press of doctors prescribing 'medical' marijuana to patients in California found that beyond a medical license, the physicians do not need to have any relevant training, familiarity with the scientific literature on pot's benefit and side-effects or special certification. There are no reporting requirements and no central database to track doctors or patients. Researchers identified 233 of these doctors and checked the names against state medical board files, finding that most doctors prescribing marijuana had clean records. However, researchers found that 68 physicians had blemished records. Some of the disciplinary actions against them included fraud, incorrectly prescribing drugs, misuse of prescription or illicit drugs, and negligence. They also found:
  - A San Francisco doctor who received four years probation after she failed to heed a psychiatrist's request to reconsider her marijuana recommendation to a 19-year-old patient suffering from depression. The patient committed suicide six months later. The doctor now operates medical marijuana practices in eight cities.
  - A Glendale obstetrician-gynecologist who pleaded guilty last year to billing Medicare for $77,000 worth of diagnostic tests he never performed while working in Texas. Since moving to Los Angeles, he helped set up pot evaluation offices in 11 locations.
  - A Fresno osteopath who was arrested in June 2008 for driving under the influence of alcohol and whose urine tested positive for marijuana, anti-anxiety drugs and a prescription stimulant. Two months later he was arrested again for driving with a suspended license, and involuntarily hospitalized as a suicide risk. He was convicted in both cases, and DEA revoked his license to prescribe narcotics. He is now giving pot recommendations at his private practice.[72]
- In a professional pharmacology journal, a doctor of pharmacology wrote, "The ethical quandary that I have as a pharmacist is allowing lay people to open dispensaries for profit and supply marijuana to people without any quality control over what's dispensed or accountability to those being dispensed this potent drug."[73]
- The owners of a Satellite Beach house in Brevard County, Florida were told the renters would take care of the lawn and clean the pool

themselves. What they didn't know is that they would be using the water from the swimming pool as part of the irrigation system for a hydroponic indoor marijuana grow in three of the four bedrooms of their home. "They even dug into the foundation of the house to put pipes and wires in," according to Kathleen Burgess, one of the owners, who estimated the property damage at $60,000. The Brevard County Sheriff's Office found 24 marijuana plants inside with a possible yield of 200 pounds of cannabis.[74]

- According to a Los Angeles press report, homeowners in Fair Oaks, California called the local cannabis club a "free for all." Conflicts among customers, sometimes 300 per day, had to be resolved by security guards. It was apparent that not all of the customers were legitimate patients. Even Dr. Charles Moser, a local physician who voted for Prop 215, said that he "… saw people coming up on bikes and skateboards, with backpacks, healthy-looking young men."[75]

The Consequences of Marijuana Grows

- In addition to problems with the cannabis clubs themselves, California residents are also complaining about marijuana grows that supply the clubs. In Willits, California, residents and officials pointed out numerous problems, including the side-effects of resin from a cannabis growing operation that affected residents' health. Additionally, residents complained about the influx of homeless people looking for work at marijuana harvest time. "Since this medical marijuana thing our town has gone to hell," said Jolene Carrillo. "Every year we have all these creepy people. They sleep behind the Safeway and Rays and go to the bathroom there. They go to Our Daily Bread and eat the food poor people need."[76]
- In the city of Arcata, California, LaVina Collenberg discovered that the nice young gentleman who rented her home on the outskirts of town was using it to grow marijuana after a neighbor called to tell her the house was on fire. In the charred remains she found grow lights, 3-foot-high marijuana plants, seeds germinating in the spa, air vents cut through the roof, and water from the growing operation soaking the carpeting and sub-flooring. Fire Protection District Chief John McFarland says "that most local structural fires involve marijuana cultivation." "Law enforcement officials estimate that 1,000 of the

7,500 homes in this Humboldt County community are being used to cultivate marijuana, slashing into the housing stock, spreading building-safety problems and sowing neighborhood discord."[77]

- "Arcata Mayor Mark Wheetley said that marijuana growing has become a quality-of-life issue in this town of 17,000. People from all camps say enough is enough. It is like this renegade Wild West mentality." Humboldt State University President Rollin Richmond is concerned that "so many houses have been converted into pot farms that the availability of student rentals has been reduced and the community's aura of marijuana is turning off some prospective students. My own sense is that people are abusing Proposition 215 to allow them to use marijuana…as recreational drugs."[78]

- A couple in Altadena, California bought their first home, what seemed to be a buyers dream, with fresh paint, carpet and fixtures. After they moved in their dream house became a nightmare. The smell of fresh paint was overtaken by the smell of stachybotrys mold growing throughout the house, forcing them to move and spend over $42,000 in repairs. Months later an electrical fire put them out again. The mold, bad wiring, and gas leaks all stemmed from the undisclosed past of the house as a marijuana grow.[79]

- Marijuana grows also hurt the environment. In October 2010 the state Department of Fish and Game wardens in California discussed recent cases involving the diversion of water from creeks. "When people divert water from creeks they deprive wildlife of its most basic water need," said DFG warden and spokesman Patrick Foy. "(Growers) also allow chemicals needed for cultivation to drain back onto the creek…poisoning everything downstream for who knows how long. We walk upstream to find out why the fish have died, and more often now than 25 years ago, we're finding the cause is marijuana gardens," Foy said.[80]

The detection and dismantling of these operations have become increasingly dangerous through the introduction and presence of firearms and "booby-traps" deployed to protect their capital investment. In addition, Mexican drug trafficking organizations (DTO) have realized that the lucrative California marijuana cultivation business eliminates the need to breach the southern border with contraband. The DTOs have tapped the expanding and voracious consumer appetite through outlets provided by the dispensaries, generating millions of dollars in cash which is easily smuggled south of the border back to the DTOs.

A marked increase in narco-terrorism throughout Mexico has been driven, in part, by the kidnapping and forced servitude of Mexican nationals in working the illicit cultivation operations in northern California (and elsewhere) to avoid retribution to themselves or extended families by the DTOs.

Many drug users are taking advantage of the guise of "compassionate care" to obtain and sell marijuana for non-medical use.

- In Great Falls, Montana, school counselors are seeing an increase in the use of marijuana by students. According to Earlene Ostberg, a school Chemical Awareness/Responsive Education Counselor, most of the students that are failing are smoking pot. "When I ask 'why,' a lot of kids are real defensive. They say "Mrs. Ostberg, it's medicinal. I could get a green (medical marijuana) card."[81]

- "The owner of six Los Angeles-area medical marijuana dispensaries was arrested by federal agents ... after an investigation sparked by a traffic accident in which a motorist high on one of the dispensaries' products plowed into a parked SUV, killing the driver and paralyzing a California Highway Patrol Officer." The driver had a large amount of marijuana and marijuana edibles in his pickup truck, purchased from the Holistic Caregivers facility in Compton. The owner, Virgil Grant, had an expired business license to operate an herbal retail store. In another of his dispensaries an employee was observed selling $5,700 worth of marijuana out the back door. Mr. Grant, who had previous convictions on drugs and weapons related-offenses, has been "charged with drug conspiracy, money laundering, and operating a drug-involved premise within 1,000 feet of a school."[82]

- A *Rolling Stone* article describes the "wink and nod" given to customers seeking marijuana for non-medical purposes by some dispensaries. "At the counter, a guy in a USC shirt is talking to the goateed clerk (Daniel's employees are paid approximately twenty dollars per hour, *plus a free gram per day*). With all the options, the customer --er, patient --doesn't know what to buy." "The muffins look nice," he says. "They're about a gram and a half of hash, which is pretty good," says the clerk. Then he points to the goo --superpotent powdery hash mixed with honey. "This is what you want," he says. "This will definitely get you medicated."[83]

- A Santa Cruz, California man, Edwin Hoey, was arrested in December, 2006. Deputies found 100 pounds of marijuana at his residence during an investigation. His attorney claimed that his client was providing pot for local medical marijuana dispensaries. However, law enforcement found among his possessions more than $500,000 in cash and a French wine collection valued at $150,000. Investigators found that Mr. Hoey was making a big profit from medical pot, some of which he sold to non-medicinal customers on the East Coast.[84]

- Two East County (California) teenagers were suspended for showing up at school high, with a medical marijuana card as their excuse.[85]

- A news article reports the ease with which patients are able to obtain medical marijuana. Primary caregivers are authorized by law to grow, transport and provide marijuana to patients. Caregivers do not need any background in health care to hold this status, and they are not required to register with the state. All it takes is an oral or written agreement between the caregiver and a patient designating you as their primary caregiver.[86]

- *Rolling Stone* magazine reported on abuses associated with Proposition 215. "... business is good for ...compassionate caregivers, freedom fighters, botanists in love with the art of growing, Long Beach homeys, Valley Boys, Oakland thugs, and even one savvy gal who wants her girlfriends to sell medical marijuana while wearing pasties. But as in any drug business, a criminal element persists—storage lockers of product, safes of cash, hustlers trying to rob those lockers and safes, guns to protect one from the hustlers, and the constant risk of arrest."[87]

- A news reporter for the Santa Cruz *Sentinel* interviewed a defense attorney who acknowledged that he turns away clients who admit they have taken advantage of the law to use marijuana for non-medical purposes. "These people aren't sick... and are simply trying to hide behind the Compassionate Use Act for recreational or profit-making reasons." This lawyer estimates that up to 30 percent of those seeking his assistance are involved with marijuana for non-medical uses.[88]

Because of abuses associated with the cannabis clubs, law enforcement and localities have cracked down on these fronts for marijuana dealers.

- In Montana, where voters approved "medical" marijuana in 2004, there has been a recent influx of registered "medical" marijuana cardholders. As of June 2009 there were only 2,923 cardholders; now there are approximately 15,000 cardholders. As a result of this increase, there has been a proliferation of storefront dispensaries, with an increase from 919 to over 5,000. The existing law does not have the proper regulations to manage these businesses and ensure public safety.[89]

- In Billings, the City Council approved a six-month moratorium on new medical businesses in May 2010 after two evenings of violence against dispensaries. They also ordered the closure of 25 of the 81 dispensaries for not being properly registered with the state.[90]

- In Kalispell, they recently banned any new "medical" marijuana stores in the city following the bludgeoning death of a patient that authorities believe was related to the theft of "medical" marijuana plants.[91]

- In April 2010 the principal and counselors from Great Falls High School testified that teenagers are smoking more marijuana than ever before. Principal Dick Kloppel stated that "I firmly believe it is directly attributable to the increased availability of the drug through caregivers and cardholders."[92]

- Mikie Messman, Chemical Awareness/Responsive Education Coordinator for the school district testified that the students told her that marijuana relieves their stress. Instead of learning how to cope with stress, they are covering it up. "These kids are using it as medication so they don't have to deal with adolescence," Messman said.[93]

- In response to the information provided by school personnel and others who testified, in June 2010 Great Falls city commissioners voted to ban medical marijuana businesses from the city.[94]

- A block from the state capitol in Helena, the Cannabis Caregivers Network, set up a cannabis caravan, a makeshift clinic, using a band of doctors and medical marijuana advocates roaming Montana to sign up thousands of patients to become "medical" marijuana cardholders. For $150 patients see a doctor who provides a recommendation that they be allowed to buy and smoke "medical" marijuana. The Montana Medical Board has been working to curtail the practice of such mass screenings. They recently fined a doctor who participated in a similar clinic for seeing 150 patients in 14 and 1/2 hours, or approximately a patient every six minutes. There was no way a thorough examination, a medical history, discussion of alternative treatments and oversight of the patients could have occurred.[95]

- One caravan recently ran a clinic in a hotel in Helena, where they processed between 200 and 300 people seeking a doctor's recommendation. The group then assisted the patient with sending the application and doctor's recommendation to the state health department. Afterwards patients were ushered into another room where half a dozen marijuana providers competed for their business.[96]

- In November 2010 the Montana Board of Medical Examiners stated that internet-based video examinations for people seeking approval to use medical marijuana did not meet the Board's standards and requires that doctors must conduct a hands-on physical examination before signing off on someone receiving "medical" marijuana.[97]

- Although Colorado approved the use of "medical" marijuana in 2000, it wasn't until 2009 that dispensaries began to proliferate throughout the state and the medical marijuana card registry grew by the thousands.

  - In order to avoid the problems experienced by other states, legislators wrote bills to regulate the industry. In June 2010 Governor Bill Ritter signed House Bill 1284, which requires that dispensaries be licensed at the state and local level, and still allows localities to ban them. He also signed Senate Bill 109, which requires doctors who recommend medical marijuana to complete a full assessment of the patient's medical history, discuss their medical condition, and be available for follow-up care.[98]

  - The State's Senior Director of Enforcement at the Department of Revenue, Matt Cook, was put in charge of drawing up a stringent regulation scheme that aims to turn the industry into a legitimate enterprise. "We plan to track the entire commodity from the seed to the sale. We will see virtually everything from the time a seed goes into the ground to the time the plants are harvested, cultivated, processed, packaged, stored." Applying for a license requires completing a form detailing immediate family and personal finance history. No felons need apply. Small dispensaries will pay at least $7,500 for a license. Rules will require that at least 70 percent of the marijuana is grown there. Every jar of cannabis will have to be labeled with the chemicals used during its production. These regulations will decrease the number of dispensaries and increase public safety.[99]

- Colorado will be the first state to regulate production of medical marijuana. Right now patients have no way to verify that the product they are purchasing is what is advertised. Given that marijuana is not approved as a medicine and regulated by the FDA, nor as a legitimate crop that is overseen by the U.S. Department of Agriculture, there are no guidelines to follow.

- According to an article in Time magazine, "Owners will soon be required to place video cameras throughout the cultivation sites and dispensaries so regulators can log on to the internet and trace the movement of every marijuana bud from the moment its seeds are planted to the point of sale. The video will be transmitted to a website accessible to regulators around the clock. The regulators will dictate where the cameras must be placed and at what angle.[100] A current attempt to challenge the new regulation requiring videotaping as a violation of marijuana patients' constitutional right to privacy was rejected by the Colorado Supreme Court.[101]

- According to an article in the *Los Angeles Times*, in 2007 there were 186 marijuana dispensaries registered with the city. Recognizing that hundreds of dispensaries were proliferating across the city, the City Council imposed a moratorium on new ones until regulations are put in place. However, operators were allowed to appeal for a hardship exemption. The City Council did not grant any exemptions, but dispensaries were allowed to open. The City Council has since eliminated the hardship exemption and is proposing an ordinance that would shut down dispensaries that opened during the moratorium.[102]

- On September 10, 2009, 14 search warrants were served at 14 marijuana dispensaries and six associated residences in San Diego. According to San Diego County District Attorney Bonnie M. Dumanis, "these so-called 'marijuana dispensaries' are nothing more than for-profit storefront drug dealing operations run by drug dealers hiding behind the state's medical marijuana law." For profit marijuana dispensaries are not legal according to state law. "We have not, and will not prosecute people who are legitimately and legally using medical marijuana." Residents living near some of the storefronts complained to law enforcement and local government about the increase in crimes associated with the dispensaries and about their proximity to schools and areas frequented by children.[103]

- On November 13, 2009 the Los Angeles City Attorney's Office submitted a new draft medical marijuana ordinance for council to review.[104]
- On November 18, 2009, Los Angeles County District Attorney Steve Cooley warned the Los Angeles City Council that he intends to prosecute dispensaries that sell drugs even if the city's leaders decide to allow those transactions. DA Cooley said that "state laws do not allow medical marijuana to be sold." Both Cooley and City Attorney Carmen Trutanich agree that recent court decisions clearly state that collectives cannot sell marijuana over the counter, but can be reimbursed for the cost of growing the marijuana.[105] Los Angeles County Superior Court Judge James C. Chalfant agreed that state law does not allow medical marijuana to be sold. "I don't believe that a storefront dispensary that sells marijuana is lawful."[106]
- In February 2010, District Attorney Steve Cooley charged Jeff Joseph, operator of a Culver City dispensary with 24 felonies, including selling and transporting marijuana, and money laundering. In addition, the Los Angeles City Attorney's office has joined in a civil lawsuit against Joseph and two other dispensaries, charging that they are public nuisances and are operating illegally.[107]
- In January 2010 the Los Angeles City Council adopted a comprehensive medical marijuana ordinance that enforces strict controls on dispensaries, forcing hundreds of shops to close. Although the ordinance sets the limit to 70, the number would be closer to 150 by allowing those registered with the city in 2007 to remain. New requirements include banning consumption at the dispensary and not locating within 1,000 feet of schools, parks, libraries and other dispensaries.[108]
- In May 2010 the Los Angeles city prosecutors began notifying 439 dispensaries that they had to shut down by June 7, 2010. Property owners and dispensary operators were sent letters informing them that violations could lead to six months in jail and a $1,000 fine. Additional civil penalties could be added.[109]
- "In Mendocino County, where plants grow more than 15 feet high, medical marijuana clubs adopt stretches of highway, and the sticky, sweet aroma of cannabis fills this city's streets during the autumn

harvest,...residents are wondering if the state's embrace of marijuana for medicinal purpose has gone too far....Some residents and law enforcement officials say the California law has increasingly and unintentionally provided legal cover for large-scale marijuana growers – and the problems such big-money operations can attract." On June 3, 2008, the County passed Measure B, which reduced the number of plants allowed to be grown. Numerous initiatives like these throughout the state demonstrate that residents want to see more, not less, regulation of the medical marijuana program.[110]

- In March, 2006, DEA worked with state and local law enforcement to dismantle the largest marijuana-laced candy manufacturing organization in the western United States. The five-month investigation resulted in the arrest of the organization's leader and the seizure of more than 4,000 marijuana plants, $100,000 in U.S. currency, three firearms, and hundreds of marijuana-laced food products. The marijuana-laced products, packaged to mimic legitimate food products, included labels such as "Buddafingers," "Munchy Way," and "Pot Tarts." The items were packaged in large boxes for distribution to cannabis clubs throughout the West Coast and over the Internet.

- Many cities and counties in California have refused to allow cannabis clubs to operate, despite the passage of Proposition 215. One hundred and forty-two cities and 12 counties have banned cannabis clubs outright; 14 counties and 102 cities have moratoria against them; 42 cities and nine counties have ordinances regulating them.[111]

- In San Francisco, things got so out of control that Mayor Gavin Newsom had to close many of the "clinics" because drug addicts were clustering around them, causing fear among city residents.[112]

DANGERS OF MARIJUANA

Marijuana Is Dangerous to the User and Others

Legalization of marijuana, no matter how it begins, will come at the expense of our children and public safety. It will create dependency and treatment issues, and open the door to use of other drugs, impaired health, delinquent behavior, and drugged drivers.

This is not the marijuana of the 1970s; today's marijuana is far more powerful On May 14, 2009, analysis from the National Institute on Drug Abuse (NIDA)-funded University of Mississippi's Potency Monitoring Project revealed that marijuana potency levels in the U.S. are the highest ever reported since the scientific analysis of the drug began.

- According to the latest data, the average amount of THC in seized samples has reached 10.1 percent. This compares to an average of just under four percent reported in 1983 and represents more than a doubling of the potency of the drug since that time.[113]
- NIDA Director Dr. Nora Volkow stated that, "Although the overall number of young people using marijuana has declined in recent years, there is still reason for great concern, particularly since roughly 60 percent of first-time marijuana users are under 18 years old. During adolescence and into young adulthood, the brain continues to develop and may be vulnerable to marijuana's deleterious effects. Science has shown that marijuana can produce adverse physical, mental, emotional, and behavioral changes, and contrary to popular belief--it can be addictive."[114]

Skunk, the more potent form of marijuana being used in the United Kingdom today, contains 15 to 20 percent THC, and new resin preparations have up to 30 percent.[115]

Increasingly, the international community is joining the United States in recognizing the fallacy of arguments claiming marijuana use is a harmless activity with no consequences to others.

- Antonio Maria Costa, then Executive Director of the United Nations Office on Drugs and Crime, noted in an article published in *The Independent on Sunday* "The debate over the drug is no longer about liberty; it's about health." He continued, "Evidence of the damage to mental health caused by cannabis use—from loss of concentration to paranoia, aggressiveness and outright psychosis—is mounting and cannot be ignored. Emergency-room admissions involving cannabis is rising, as is demand for rehabilitation treatment. ...It is time to explode the myth of cannabis as a 'soft' drug."[116]
- As ONDCP Director R. Gil Kerlikowske noted, "The concern with marijuana is not born out of any culture war mentality, but out of what science tells us about the drug's effects."[117]

Mental Health Issues Related to Marijuana

There is mounting evidence that use of marijuana, particularly by adolescents, can lead to serious mental health problems.

- "Nearly one in ten first-year college students at a mid-Atlantic university have a cannabis use disorder (CUD) according to a NIDA-funded study of drug use conducted by investigators from the Center for Substance Abuse Research at the University of Maryland." "Students who had used cannabis five or more times in the past year – regardless of whether or not they met the criteria for CUD – reported problems related to their cannabis use, such as concentration problems (40.1 percent), regularly putting themselves in physical danger (24.3 percent), and driving after using marijuana (18.6 percent)."[118]
- According to a recent report by the Office of National Drug Control Policy on teens, depression and marijuana use: [119]
  - Depressed teens are twice as likely as non-depressed teens to use marijuana and other illicit drugs.
  - Depressed teens are more than twice as likely as their peers to abuse or become dependent on marijuana.
  - Marijuana use can worsen depression and lead to more serious mental illness such as schizophrenia, anxiety, and even suicide.
  - Teens who smoke marijuana at least once a month are three times more likely to have suicidal thoughts than non-users.
  - The percentage of depressed teens is equal to the percentage of depressed adults, but depressed teens are more likely than depressed adults to use marijuana than other drugs.
- According to a recent Australian study, there is now conclusive evidence that smoking cannabis hastens the appearance of psychotic illnesses by up to three years. Dr. Mathew Large from the University of New South Wales reports that"…in addition to early cannabis smoking bringing on schizophrenia it brings it on early by an average of 2.7 years early – earlier than you would have otherwise developed it had you not been a cannabis smoker. The risks for older people is about a doubling of the risk." "For young people who smoke cannabis regularly, instead of having around a one percent chance of developing schizophrenia during their life they will end up with something like a five percent chance of developing schizophrenia." Philip Mitchell, head of Psychiatry at the University stated that while

"this research can't distinguish about whether cannabis causes schizophrenia or brings it out in vulnerable people…it makes it very clear that cannabis is playing a significant role in psychosis."[120]

- Researchers from the University of Oulu in Finland interviewed over 6,000 youth ages 15 and 16 and found that "teenage cannabis users are more likely to suffer psychotic symptoms and have a greater risk of developing schizophrenia in later life."[121]

- Australian researchers report that long-term, heavy cannabis use may be associated with structural abnormalities in areas of the brain which govern memory, emotion, and aggression. Brain scans showed that the hippocampus was 12 percent smaller and the amygdale 7 percent smaller in men who smoked at least 5 cigarettes daily for almost 10 years. Dr. Mura Yucel, the lead researcher stated that "this new evidence plays an important role in further understanding the effects of marijuana and its impact on brain functions. The study is the first to show that long-term cannabis use can adversely affect all users, not just those in the high-risk categories such as the young, or those susceptible to mental illness, as previously thought."[122]

- A two-year study by the National Cannabis Prevention and Information Centre, at the University of New South Wales in Sydney, Australia found that cannabis users can be as aggressive as crystal methamphetamine users, with almost one in four men and one in three women being violent toward hospital staff or injuring themselves after acting aggressively. Almost 12 percent were considered a suicide risk. The head of the Emergency Department at St. Vincent's Hospital, Gordian Fulde, said "that most people still believed marijuana was a soft drug, but the old image of feeling sleepy and having the munchies after you've smoked is entirely inappropriate for modern-day marijuana. With hydroponic cannabis, the levels of THC can be tenfold what they are in normal cannabis so we are seeing some very, very serious fallout."[123]

- A study published in the March 2008 Journal of the American Academy of Child and Adolescent Psychiatry cited the harm of smoking marijuana during pregnancy. The study found a significant relationship between marijuana exposure and child intelligence. Researchers concluded that "prenatal marijuana exposure has a significant effect on school-age intellectual development."[124]

- Doctors at Yale University documented marijuana's damaging effect on the brain after nearly half of 150 healthy volunteers experienced psychotic symptoms, including hallucinations and paranoid delusions, when given THC, the drug's primary active ingredient. The findings were released during a May 2007 international health conference in London.[125]

- U.S. scientists have discovered that the active ingredient in marijuana interferes with synchronized activity between neurons in the hippocampus of rats. The authors of this November 2006 study suggest that action of tetrahydrocannabinol, or THC, might explain why marijuana impairs memory.[126]

- A pair of articles in the *Canadian Journal of Psychiatry* reflects that cannabis use can trigger schizophrenia in people already vulnerable to the mental illness and assert that this fact should shape marijuana policy.[127]

- Memory, speed of thinking, and other cognitive abilities get worse over time with marijuana use, according to a new study published in the March 14, 2006 issue of *Neurology*, the scientific journal of the American Academy of Neurology. The study found that frequent marijuana users performed worse than non-users on tests of cognitive abilities, including divided attention and verbal fluency. Those who had used marijuana for 10 years or more had more problems with their thinking abilities than those who had used marijuana for 5-to-10 years. All of the marijuana users were heavy users, which was defined as smoking four or more joints per week.[128]

- John Walters, then the Director of the Office of National Drug Control Policy, Charles G. Curie, then the Administrator of the Substance Abuse and Mental Health Services Administration, and experts and scientists from leading mental health organizations joined together in May 2005 to warn parents about the mental health dangers marijuana poses to teens. According to several recent studies, marijuana use has been linked with depression and suicidal thoughts, in addition to schizophrenia. These studies report that weekly marijuana use among teens doubles the risk of developing depression and triples the incidence of suicidal thoughts.[129]

- Dr. Andrew Campbell, a member of the New South Wales (Australia) Mental Health Review Tribunal, published a study in 2005 which revealed that four out of five individuals with schizophrenia were regular cannabis users when they were teenagers. Between 75-80 per cent of the patients involved in the study used cannabis habitually between the ages of 12 and 21.[130] In addition, a laboratory-controlled study by Yale scientists, published in 2004, found that THC "transiently induced a range of schizophrenia-like effects in healthy people."[131]

- Carleton University researchers published a study in 2005 showing that current marijuana users who smoke at least five "joints" per week did significantly worse than non-users when tested on neurocognition tests such as processing speed, memory, and overall IQ.[132]

- Robin Murray, a professor of psychiatry at London's Institute of Psychiatry and consultant at the Maudsley Hospital in London, wrote an editorial which appeared in *The Independence on Sunday*, on March 18, 2007, in which he states that the British Government's "mistake was rather to give the impression that cannabis was harmless and that there was no link to psychosis." Based on the fact that "…in the late 1980s and 1990s psychiatrists like me began to see growing numbers of young people with schizophrenia who were taking large amounts of cannabis" Murray claims that "…at least 10 percent of all people with schizophrenia in the UK would not have developed the illness if they had not smoked cannabis." By his estimates, 25,000 individuals have ruined their lives because they smoked cannabis. He also points out that the "skunk" variety of cannabis, which is very popular among young people in Great Britain, contains "15 to 20 percent THC, and new resin preparations have up to 30 percent."[133]

- Dr. John MacLeod, a prominent British psychiatrist states: "If you assume such a link (to schizophrenia with cannabis) then the number of cases of schizophrenia will increase significantly in line with increased use of the drug." He predicts that cannabis use may account for a quarter of all new cases of schizophrenia in three years' time.[134]

- A study by Scientists at the Queensland Brain Institute in Australia on long-term marijuana use and the increased risk of psychosis confirms earlier findings. "Compared with those who had never used cannabis, young adults who had six or more years since first use of cannabis were twice as likely to develop a non-affective psychosis (such as schizophrenia), " McGrath wrote in a study published in the Archives of General Psychiatry Journal. "They were also four times as likely to have high scores in clinical tests of delusion."[135]

- According to Margaret Trudeau, "Marijuana can trigger psychosis." "Quitting cannabis has been an important part of my recovery from mental illness," Margaret Trudeau, ex-wife of former Canadian prime Minister Pierre Trudeau, reported at a press conference at the

Canadian Mental Health Conference in Vancouver on February 15, 2007. "Every time I was hospitalized it was preceded by heavy marijuana use."[136]

- A study by doctors from the National Institute of Drug Abuse found that people who smoked marijuana had changes in the blood flow in their brains even after a month of not smoking. The marijuana users had PI (pulsatility index) values somewhat higher than people with chronic high blood pressure and diabetes, which suggests that marijuana use leads to abnormalities in the small blood vessels in the brain. These findings could explain in part the problems with thinking and remembering found in other studies of marijuana users.[137]

- In a presentation on "Neuroimaging Marijuana Use and Effects on Cognitive Function" Professor Krista Lisdahl Medina suggests that chronic heavy marijuana use during adolescence is associated with poorer performance on thinking tasks, including slower psychomotor speed and poorer complex attention, verbal memory and planning ability. "While recent findings suggest partial recovery of verbal memory functioning within the first three weeks of adolescent abstinence from marijuana, complex attention skills continue to be affected. Not only are their thinking abilities worse, their brain activation to cognitive task is abnormal."[138]

Physical Health Issues Related to Marijuana

Marijuana use also affects the physical health of users.

- Under the Safe Drinking Water and Toxic Enforcement Act of 1986, the Governor of California is required to revise and republish at least once a year the list of chemicals known to the state to cause cancer or reproductive toxicity. On September 11, 2009, the California Environmental Protection Agency, Office of Environmental Health Hazard Assessment, published the latest list. The list includes a new chemical added in June, marijuana smoke, and lists cancer as the type of toxicity.[139]

- A study by researchers at the Erasmus University Medical Center in Rotterdam, Netherlands found woman who smoked pot during pregnancy may impair their baby's growth and development in the womb. The babies born to marijuana users tended to weigh less and have smaller heads than other infants, both of which are linked to increased risk of problems with thinking, memory, and behavioral problems in childhood.[140]

- A long-term study of over 900 New Zealanders by the University of Otago, New Zealand School of Dentistry has found that "heavy marijuana use has been found to contribute to gum disease, apart from the known effects that tobacco smoke was already known to have."[141]

- A study from Monash University and the Alfred Hospital in Australia has found that "bullous lung disease occurs in marijuana smokers 20 years earlier than tobacco smokers. Often caused by exposure to toxic chemicals or long-term exposure to tobacco smoke, bullae is a condition where air trapped in the lungs causes obstruction to breathing and eventual destruction of the lungs." Dr. Matthew Naughton explains that "marijuana is inhaled as extremely hot fumes to the peak inspiration and held for as long as possible before slow exhalation. This predisposes to greater damage to the lungs and makes marijuana smokers more prone to bullous disease as compared to cigarette smokers."[142]

- In December 2007 researchers in Canada reported that "marijuana smoke contains significantly higher levels of toxic compounds -- including ammonia and hydrogen cyanide --than tobacco smoke and may therefore pose similar health risks." "Ammonia levels were 20 times higher in the marijuana smoke than in the tobacco smoke, while hydrogen cyanide, nitric oxide and certain aromatic amines occurred at levels 3-5 times higher in the marijuana smoke."[143]

- Marijuana worsens breathing problems in current smokers with chronic obstructive pulmonary disease (COPD), according to a study released by the American Thoracic Society in May 2007. Among people age 40 and older, smoking cigarettes and marijuana together boosted the odds of developing COPD to 3.5 times the risk of someone who smoked neither.[144]

- Scientists at Sweden's Karolinska Institute, a medical university, have advanced their understanding of how smoking marijuana during pregnancy may damage the fetal brain. Findings from their study, released in May 2007, explain how endogenous cannabinoids exert adverse effects on nerve cells, potentially imposing life-long cognitive and motor deficits in afflicted new born babies.[145]

- A study from New Zealand reports that cannabis smoking may cause five percent of lung cancer cases in that country. Dr. Sarah Aldington of the Medical Research Institute in Wellington presented her study results at the Thoracic Society conference in Auckland on March 26, 2007.[146]

- Researchers at the Fred Hutchinson Cancer Research Center in Seattle found that frequent or long-term marijuana use may significantly increase a man's risk of developing the most aggressive type of testicular cancer, nonseminoma. Nonseminoma is a fast-growing testicular malignancy that tends to strike early, between the ages of 20 and 35, and accounts for about 40 percent of all testicular-cancer cases. Dr. Stephen Schwartz stated that researchers are still studying the long-term health consequences of marijuana smoking, especially heavy marijuana smoking and "in the absence of more certain information, a decision to smoke marijuana recreationally means that one is taking a chance on one's future health."[147]

- According to the 2009 Drug Abuse Warning Network (DAWN), there were 973,591emergency department (ED) visits involving an illicit drug. Marijuana was involved in376,467 of these visits, second only to cocaine.[148]

- Among ED visits made by patients aged 20 or younger resulting in drug misuse or abuse, after alcohol, marijuana was the most commonly involved illicit drug (125.3 visits per 100,100).[149]

- On an average day in 2008 there were 723 drug related ED visits for youth 12 to17 years of age. Of those visits, 129 involved marijuana.[150]

- According to researchers at the Yale School of Medicine, long-term exposure to marijuana smoke is linked to many of the same kinds of health problems as those experienced by long-term cigarette smokers. "...[C]linicians should advise their patients of the potential negative impact of marijuana smoking on overall lung health."[151]

- While smoking cigarettes is known to be a major risk factor for the bladder cancer most common among people age 60 and older, researchers are now finding a correlation between smoking marijuana and bladder cancer. In a study of younger patients with transitional cell bladder cancer, Dr. Martha Terriss found that 88.5 percent had a history of smoking marijuana. Marijuana smoke has many of the same carcinogen-containing tars as cigarettes and may get even more into the body because marijuana cigarettes are unfiltered and users tend to hold the smoke in their lungs for prolonged periods. Dr. Terriss notes that more research is needed, but does recommend that when doctors find blood in a young patient's urine sample, they may want to include questions about marijuana use in their follow-up[152]

- Smoking marijuana can cause changes in lung tissue that may promote cancer growth, according to a review of decades of research on marijuana smoking and lung cancer. However, it is not possible to directly link pot use to lung cancer based on existing evidence. Nevertheless, researchers indicate that the precancerous changes seen in studies included in their analysis, as well as the fact that marijuana smokers generally inhale more deeply and hold smoke in their lungs longer than cigarette smokers, and that marijuana is smoked without a filter, do suggest that smoking pot could indeed boost lung cancer risk. It is known, they add, that marijuana smoking deposits more tar in the lungs than cigarette smoking does.[153]

- Smoking three cannabis joints will cause you to inhale the same amount of toxic chemicals as a whole pack of cigarettes according to researchers from the French National Consumers' Institute. Cannabis smoke contains seven times more tar and carbon monoxide than cigarette smoke. Someone smoking a joint of cannabis resin rolled with tobacco will inhale twice the amount of benzene and three times as much toluene as if they were smoking a regular cigarette.[154]

- According to research, the use of marijuana by women trying to conceive or those recently becoming pregnant is not recommended, as it endangers the passage of the embryo from the ovary to the uterus and can result in a failed pregnancy. The researchers from Vanderbilt University say a study with mice has shown that marijuana exposure may compromise the pregnancy outcome because an active ingredient in marijuana, tetrahydrocannabinol (THC), interferes with a fertilized egg's ability to implant in the lining of the uterus.[155]

- Infants exposed to marijuana in the womb show subtle behavioral changes in their first days of life, according to researchers in Brazil. The newborns were more irritable than non-exposed infants, less responsive, and more difficult to calm. They also cried more, startled more easily, and were jitterier. Such changes have the potential to interfere with the mother-child bonding process. "It is necessary to counter the misconception that marijuana is a 'benign drug' and to educate women regarding the risks and possible consequences related to its use during pregnancy," Dr. Marina Carvahlo de Moraes Barros and her colleagues concluded.[156]

• Marijuana smoking has been implicated as a causative factor in tumors of the head and neck and of the lung. The marijuana smokers in whom these tumors occur are usually much younger than the tobacco smokers who are the usual victims of these malignancies. Although a recent study published by the Medical College of Georgia and Stanford University suggests a causal relationship between marijuana exposure and bladder cancer, larger scale epidemiologic and basic science studies are needed to confirm the role of marijuana smoking as an etiologic agent in the development of transitional cell carcinoma.[157]

• According to a 2005 study of marijuana's long-term pulmonary effects by Dr. Donald Tashkin at the University of California, Los Angeles, marijuana smoking deposits significantly more tar and known carcinogens within the tar, such a polycyclic aromatic hydrocarbons, into the airways. In addition to precancerous changes, marijuana smoking is associated with impaired function of the immune system components in the lungs.[158]

• Smoked marijuana has also been associated with an increased risk of the same respiratory symptoms as tobacco, including coughing, phlegm production, chronic bronchitis, shortness of breath and wheezing. Because cannabis plants are contaminated with a range of fungal spores, smoking marijuana may also increase the risk of respiratory exposure by infectious organisms (i.e., molds and fungi).[159]

• Marijuana takes the risks of tobacco and raises them. Marijuana smoke contains more than 400 chemicals and increases the risk of serious health consequences, including lung damage.[160]

• An April 2007 article published by the *Harm Reduction Journal,* and funded by the pro-legalization Marijuana Policy Project, argues that the use of a vaporizer has the potential to reduce the danger of cannabis as far as respiratory symptoms are concerned. While these claims remain scientifically unproven, serious negative consequences still remain. For example, driving skills are still impaired, heavy adolescent use may create deviant brain structure, and 9-12 percent of cannabis users develop symptoms of dependence. A vaporizer offers no protection against these consequences.[161]

• According to two studies, marijuana use narrows arteries in the brain, "similar to patients with high blood pressure and dementia," and may explain why memory tests are difficult for marijuana users. In addition, "chronic consumers of cannabis lose molecules called CB1 receptors in the brain's arteries," leading to blood flow problems in the brain which can cause memory loss, attention deficits, and impaired learning ability.[162]

- A small study (50 patients) was conducted by the University of California San Francisco from 2003 to 2005, leading researchers to find that smoked marijuana eased HIV-related foot pain. This pain, known as peripheral neuropathy, was relieved for 52 percent of the patients in the controlled experiment. Dr. Donald Abrams, director of the study said that while subjects' pain was reduced he and his colleagues "found that adverse events, such as sedation, dizziness and confusion were significantly higher among the cannabis smokers."[163]

- In response to this study, critics of smoked marijuana were quick to point out that while THC does have some medicinal benefits, smoked marijuana is a poor delivery mechanism. Citing evidence that marijuana smoke is harmful, Dr. David Murray, chief scientist at the Office of National Drug Control Policy, noted that "People who smoke marijuana are subject to bacterial infections in the lungs...Is this really what a physician who is treating someone with a compromised immune system wants to prescribe?"[164]

    - Dr. Murray also said that the findings are "not particularly persuasive" because of the small number of subjects and the possibility that subjects knew they were smoking marijuana and had an increased expectation of efficacy. He expressed the government's support for pain relief for HIV-affected individuals and said that while "We're very much supportive of any effort to ameliorate the suffering of AIDs patients, the delivery mechanism for THC should be pills, and not smoked marijuana, which can cause lung damage and deliver varying dosages of THC."[165]

    - Researchers involved with the University of California San Francisco project admitted that there may be a problem with efforts to gauge the effects of marijuana vs. the effects of a placebo. Some users were immediately able to acknowledge that their sample was indeed cannabis because of the effects of that substance. One participant, Diana Dodson said, "I knew immediately [that I received cannabis] because I could feel the effects."[166]

- Pro-marijuana advocates were encouraged by a medical study published in *Cancer Epidemiology, Biomarkers & Prevention*. The study, published in October 2006, was based on interviews with people in Los Angeles (611 who developed lung cancer, 601 who developed cancer of the head or neck regions, and 1,040 people without cancer who were matched [to other subjects] on age, gender, and neighborhoods). The study found that people who smoke marijuana do not appear to be at increased risk of developing lung cancer.[167] While this study's findings differed from previous studies and researchers' expectations, "[o]ther experts are warning that the study should not be viewed as a green light to smoke pot, as smoking marijuana has been associated with problems such as cognitive impairment and chronic bronchitis."[168] The National Institute on Drug Abuse (NIDA) continues to maintain that smoking marijuana is detrimental to pulmonary functions.

- In its October, 2006, issue of *NIDA Notes*, mention is made of the most recent Tashkin study. "Biopsies of bronchial tissue provide evidence that regular marijuana smoking injures airway epithelial cells, leading to dysregulation of bronchial epithelial cell growth and eventually to possible malignant changes." Moreover, he adds, because marijuana smokers typically hold their breath four times as long as tobacco smokers after inhaling, marijuana smoking deposits significantly more tar and known carcinogens within the tar, such as polycyclic aromatic hydrocarbons, in the airways. In addition to precancerous changes, Dr. Tashkin found that marijuana smoking is associated with a range of damaging pulmonary effects, including inhibition of the tumor-killing and bactericidal activity of alveolar macrophages, the primary immune cells within the lung."

- NIDA also comments on the Tashkin study in the *Director's Notes* from February 2007. While acknowledging that the study concluded "that the association of these cancers with marijuana, even long-term or heavy use, is not strong and may be below practically detectable limits…these results may have been affected by selection bias or error in measuring lifetime exposure and confounder histories."[169]

- In October 2006, one of the study's authors, Dr. Hal Morgenstern, Chair of Epidemiology at the University of Michigan School of Public Health, said although the risk of cancer did not prove to be large in the recent study, "I wouldn't go so far as to say there is no increased cancer risk from smoking marijuana."[170]

Marijuana as a Precursor to Abuse of Other Drugs

- Teens who experiment with marijuana may be making themselves more vulnerable to heroin addiction later in life, if the findings from experiments with rats are any indication. "Cannabis has very long-term, enduring effects on the brain," according to Dr. Yamin Hurd of the Mount Sinai School of Medicine in New York, the study's lead author.[171]

- Marijuana is a frequent precursor to the use of more dangerous drugs and signals a significantly enhanced likelihood of drug problems in adult life. The *Journal of the American Medical Association* reported, based on a study of 300 sets of twins, "that marijuana-using twins were four times more likely than their siblings to use cocaine and crack cocaine, and five times more likely to use hallucinogens such as LSD."[172]

- Long-term studies on patterns of drug usage among young people show that very few of them use other drugs without first starting with marijuana. For example, one study found that among adults (age 26 and older) who had used cocaine, 62 percent had initiated marijuana use before age 15. By contrast, less than one percent of adults who never tried marijuana went on to use cocaine.[173]

- Columbia University's National Center on Addiction and Substance Abuse (CASA) reports that teens who used marijuana at least once in the last month are 13 times likelier than other teens to use another drug like cocaine, heroin, or methamphetamine and almost 26 times likelier than those teens who have never used marijuana to use another drug.[174]

- In the March 2007 report on substance abuse at America's colleges and universities, CASA notes that between 1993 and 2005, the proportion of students who were daily marijuana users increased 110.5 percent, from 1.9 percent to 4.0 percent (approximately 310,000 students.)[175]

- Marijuana use in early adolescence is particularly ominous. Adults who were early marijuana users were found to be five times more likely to become dependent on any drug, eight times more likely to use cocaine in the future, and fifteen times more likely to use heroin later in life.[176]

- In 2009, an estimated 14.2 percent of past year marijuana users aged 12 or older used marijuana on 300 or more days within the past 12 months.[177]
- In 2009, 4 million Americans aged 12 or older used marijuana daily or almost daily in the past year.[178]
- In 2009, an estimated 36.7 percent or 6.1 million of past month users aged 12 or older used the drug on 20 or more days in the past month.[179]
- In 2009, there were 2.4 million persons who had used marijuana for the first time within the past 12 months; this averages to approximately 6,500 initiates per day.[180]
- On an average day in 2008, 3,695 adolescents 12 to 17 years of age used marijuana for the first time. On an average day in the past year, 563,182 used marijuana.[181]
- Healthcare workers, legal counsel, police and judges indicate that marijuana is a typical precursor to methamphetamine. For instance, Nancy Kneeland, a substance abuse counselor in Idaho, pointed out that "in almost all cases meth users began with alcohol and pot."[182]

DEPENDENCY AND TREATMENT

- "The basic rule with any drug is if the drug becomes more available in the society, there will be more use of the drug," said Thomas Crowley, a University of Colorado psychiatry professor and director of the university's Division of Substance Dependence.
  "And as use expands, there will be more people who have problems with the drug."[183]
- A study of substance abuse treatment admissions in the United States between 1998 and 2008, found that although admission rates for alcohol treatment were declining, admission rates per 100,000 population for illicit drug use were increasing. One consistent pattern in every region was the increase in the admission rate for marijuana use which rose 30 percent nationally.[184]
- California, a national leader in 'medical' marijuana use, saw admission for treatment for marijuana dependence more than double over the past decade.

Admissions grew from 52 admissions per 100,000 population in 1998 to 113 per 100,000 in 2008, an increase of 117 percent.[185]

- "[R]esearch shows that use of [marijuana] can lead to dependence. Some heavy users of marijuana develop withdrawal symptoms when they have not used the drug for a period of time. Marijuana use, in fact, is often associated with behavior that meets the criteria for substance dependence established by the American Psychiatric Association."[186]

- Of the 21.8 million Americans aged 12 or older who used illicit drugs in the past 30 days in 2009, 16.7 million used marijuana, making it the most commonly used illicit drug in 2009.[187]

- Adults who first started using marijuana at or before the age of 14 are most likely to have abused or been dependent on illicit drugs in the past year.[188]

- Adults who first used marijuana at age 14 or younger were six times more likely to meet the criteria for past year illicit drug abuse or dependence than those who first used marijuana when they were 18 or older (12.6 percent vs. 2.1 percent) and almost twice as likely as those who started between the ages of 15 and 17 (12.6 percent vs. 6.6 percent).[189]

- Among all ages, marijuana was the second most common illicit drug responsible for treatment admissions in 2008 after opioids, accounting for 17 percent of all admissions--outdistancing cocaine, the next most prevalent cause.[190]

- Marijuana dependency and abuse can be moderately improved by various psychotherapy treatments, but reduced use, rather than abstinence, may be the best clinicians can hope for at this time, a new review finds.[191]

- Of all the illicit drugs, marijuana had the highest level of past-year dependence or abuse (4.3 million) in 2009.[192]

- The proportion of admissions for marijuana as the primary substance of abuse increased from 13 percent in 1998 to 17 percent in 2008.[193]

- About four in five (79 percent) of adolescent treatment admissions involved marijuana as a primary or secondary substance.[194]

DANGERS TO NON USERS

Delinquent Behaviors

Marijuana use is strongly associated with juvenile crime.

- In a 2008 paper entitled *Non-Medical Marijuana III: Rite of Passage or Russian Roulette*, CASA reported that in 2006 youth who had been arrested and booked for breaking the law were four times likelier than those who were never arrested to have used marijuana in the past year.[195]
- According to CASA in their report on *Criminal Neglect: Substance Abuse, Juvenile Justice and the Children Left Behind*, youth who use marijuana are likelier than those who do not to be arrested and arrested repeatedly. The earlier an individual begins to use marijuana, the likelier he or she is to be arrested.
- Marijuana is known to contribute to delinquent and aggressive behavior. A June 2007 report released by the White House Office of National Drug Control Policy (ONDCP) reveals that teenagers who use drugs are more likely to engage in violent and delinquent behavior. Moreover, early use of marijuana, the most commonly used drug among teens, is a warning sign for later criminal behavior. Specifically, research shows that the instances of physically attacking people, stealing property, and destroying property increase in direct proportion to the frequency with which teens smoke marijuana.[196]

In a report titled *The Relationship between Alcohol, Drug Use, and Violence among Students*, the Community Anti-Drug Coalitions of America (CADCA) reported that according to the 2006 Pride Surveys, during the 2005-2006 school year:

- Of those students who report carrying a gun to school during the 2005-2006 year, 63.9 percent report also using marijuana.
- Of those students who reported hurting others with a weapon at school, 68.4 percent had used marijuana.
- Of those students who reported being hurt by a weapon at school, 60.3 percent reported using marijuana.

- Of those students who reported threatening someone with a gun, knife, or club or threatening to hit, slap or kick someone, 27 percent reported using marijuana.
- Of those students who reported any trouble with the police, 39 percent also reported using marijuana.[197]
- According to ONDCP, the incidence of youth physically attacking others, stealing, and destroying property increased in proportion to the number of days marijuana was smoked in the past year.[198]
- ONDCP reports that marijuana users were twice as likely as non-users to report they disobeyed school rules.[199]

Drugged Drivers

- The principal concern regarding drugged driving is that driving under the influence of any drug that acts on the brain could impair one's motor skills, reaction time, and judgment. Drugged driving is a public health concern because it puts not only the driver at risk, but also passengers and others who share the road.[200]
- In Montana, where there has been an enormous increase in "medical" marijuana cardholders this past year, Narcotics Chief Mark Long told a legislative committee in April 2010 that "DUI arrests involving marijuana have skyrocketed, as have traffic fatalities where marijuana was found in the system of one of the drivers."[201]
- In 2009 there were 10.5 million persons aged 12 and older who reported driving under the influence of illicit drugs during the past year. The rate was highest among young adults aged 18 to 25.[202]
- The percentage of fatally injured drivers testing positive for drugs increased over the last five years according to data from the National Highway Traffic Safety Administration (NHTSA). In 2009, 33 percent of the 12,055 drivers fatally injured in motor vehicle crashes with known test results tested positive for at least one drug compared to 28 percent in 2005. In 2009, marijuana was the most prevalent drug found in this population – approximately 28 percent of fatally injured drivers who tested positive tested positive for marijuana.[203]
- Results from the Monitoring the Future survey indicated that in 2008 more than 12 percent of high school seniors admitted to driving under the influence of marijuana in the two weeks prior to the survey.[204]

- Recognizing that drugged driving is a serious health and safety issue, the National Organization for the Reform of Marijuana Laws (NORML) has called for a science-based educational campaign targeting drugged driving behavior. In January of 2008, Deputy Director Paul Armentano released a report titled, *Cannabis and Driving*, noting that motorists should be discouraged from driving if they have recently smoked cannabis and should never operate a motor vehicle after having consumed both marijuana and alcohol. The report also calls for the development of roadside, cannabis-sensitive technology to better assist law enforcement in identifying drivers who may be under the influence of pot.[205]

- In a 2007 National Roadside Survey of alcohol and drug use by drivers, a random sample of weekend nighttime drivers across the United States found that 16.3 percent of the drivers tested positive for drugs, compared to 2.2 percent of drivers with blood alcohol concentrations at or above the legal limit. Drugs were present more than 7 times as frequently as alcohol.[206]

- According to the National Institute of Drug Abuse (NIDA) funded study, a large number of American adolescents are putting themselves and others at great risk by driving under the influence of illicit drugs or alcohol. In 2006, 30 percent of high school seniors reported driving after drinking heavily or using drugs, or riding in a car whose driver had been drinking heavily or using drugs, as least once in the prior two weeks. Dr. Patrick O'Malley, lead author of the study, observed that "Driving under the influence is not an alcohol-only problem. In 2006, 13 percent of seniors said they drove after using marijuana while ten percent drove after having five or more drinks." "Vehicle accidents are the leading cause of death among those aged 15 to 20," added Dr. Nora Volkow, Director of NIDA. "Combining the lack of driving experience among teens with the use of marijuana and/or other substances that impair cognitive and motor abilities can be a deadly combination." [207]

- A June 2007 toxicology study conducted at the University of Maryland's Shock-Trauma Unit in Baltimore found that over 26 percent of injured drivers tested positive for marijuana. In an earlier study, the U.S. National Survey on Drug Use and Health estimated that 10.6 million Americans had driven a motor vehicle under the influence of drugs during the previous year.[208]

- In a study of seriously injured drivers admitted to a Maryland Level-1 shock-trauma center, 65.7 percent were found to have positive toxicology results for alcohol and/or drugs. Almost 51 percent of the total tested positive for illegal drugs. A total of 26.9 percent of the drivers tested positive for marijuana.[209]
- Driving under the influence of cannabis almost doubles the risk of a fatal road crash, according to a study published online by the *British Medical Journal* in December 2005. The study took place in France and involved 10,748 drivers who were involved in fatal crashes from October 2001 to September 2003. The risk of being responsible for a fatal crash increased as the blood concentration of cannabis increased. These effects were adjusted for alcohol and remained significant when also adjusted for other factors. The authors of this study assert that these results give credence to a causal relationship between cannabis and crashes.[210]
- A study of over 3000 fatally-injured drivers in Australia showed that when marijuana was present in the blood of the driver they were much more likely to be at fault for the accident. And the higher the THC concentration, the more likely they were to be culpable.[211]
- Drugged driving has become a significant problem in the United Kingdom, where almost 20 percent of drivers involved in fatal accidents had traces of drugs in their systems. The government is planning to issue roadside kits, known as "drugalysers," which will test a motorist's saliva and enable the police to identify drivers who are behind the wheel after taking illegal drugs, including marijuana.[212]
- A large shock trauma unit conducting an ongoing study found that 17 percent (one in six) of crash victims tested positive for marijuana. The rates were slightly higher for crash victims under the age of eighteen, 19 percent of who tested positive for marijuana.[213]
- The National Highway Traffic Safety Administration (NHTSA) has found that marijuana significantly impairs one's ability to safely operate a motor vehicle. According to its report, "[e]pidemiology data from road traffic arrests and fatalities indicate that after alcohol, marijuana is the most frequently detected psychoactive substance among driving populations." Problems reported include: decreased car handling performance, inability to maintain headway, impaired time and distance estimation, increased reaction times, sleepiness, lack of motor coordination, and impaired sustained vigilance.[214]

Some of the consequences of marijuana-impaired driving are startling:

- An off-duty Nevada Highway Patrol sergeant who caused a three-car crash killing a 47-year-old woman smoked marijuana a maximum of four hours before the accident. Tests showed that Sergeant Edward Lattin had 5.6 nanograms per milliliter of THC in his system before it metabolized and 26 nanograms per milliliter of THC in his blood after it was metabolized. State law allows drivers to have 2 nanograms per milliliter in their bodies before metabolizing and 5 nanograms per milliliter after it metabolizes to allow for issues such as secondhand exposure.[215]

- In Largo, Florida, a 54 year-old male driver high on marijuana struck and killed a pedestrian. A witness said that Karl Merl made no effort to avoid the 83 year old woman. Merl had 11 nanograms per milliliter of THC in his blood.[216]

- A 34 year-old male driver from Lower Paxton Township in Pennsylvania smoked marijuana and crashed his speeding car into another vehicle, killing an 87-year-old woman. Investigators of the February 2007 crash found marijuana in the driver's bloodstream, as well as partially smoked marijuana cigarettes in his car.[217]

- An 18 year-old was charged with reckless homicide in Jasper, Indiana after authorities said he crashed a pickup into a tree while under the influence of marijuana, killing his 16-year-old sister and two other teens. Authorities said the youth was under the influence of marijuana when he tried to pass another vehicle at high speed.[218]

- Police advised that a teen driver whose car veered into a school bus on August 22, 2006 in LaPorte, Michigan, was under the influence of marijuana. The teen was charged with operating while intoxicated, a Class A misdemeanor. Police said tests conducted at LaPorte Hospital detected marijuana in his bloodstream; however, since the drug can remain in the body for several weeks, the results did not show when he had used marijuana. While the teen was taken to the intensive care unit with a fracture to the upper left leg or hip, along with head injuries, none of the students on the bus were hurt.[219]

- The driver of a charter bus, whose 1999 accident resulted in the death of 22 people, had been fired from bus companies in 1989 and 1996 because he tested positive for marijuana four times. A federal investigator confirmed a report that the driver "tested positive for marijuana when he was hospitalized Sunday after the bus veered off a highway and plunged into an embankment."[220]

- In April 2002, four children and the driver of a van died when the van hit a concrete bridge abutment after veering off the freeway. Investigators reported that the children had nicknamed the driver "Smokey" because he regularly smoked marijuana. The driver was found at the crash scene with marijuana in his pocket.[221]

- A former nurse's aide was convicted in 2003 of murder and sentenced to 50 years in prison for hitting a homeless man with her car and driving home with his mangled body "lodged in the windshield." The incident happened after a night of drinking and taking drugs, including marijuana. After arriving home, the woman parked her car, with the man still lodged in the windshield, and left him there until he died.[222]

- In 2005, an eight year-old boy was killed when he was run over by an unlicensed 16-year-old driver who police believed had been smoking marijuana just before the accident.[223]

- Duane Baehler, 47, of Tulsa, Oklahoma was "involved in a fiery crash that killed his teenage son" in 2003. Police reported that Baehler had methamphetamine, cocaine and marijuana in his system at the time of the accident.[224]

OTHER CONSEQUENCES OF MARIJUANA USE

- In Massachusetts in 2009 the possession of one ounce of marijuana went from a criminal charge to a civil fine. Police and District Attorneys want residents to know that smoking weed is not a victimless crime. Middlesex District Attorney Gerard T. Leone Jr. says that he fears that "decriminalization has created a booming 'cottage industry' for dope dealers to target youths no longer fearing the stigma of arrest or how getting high could affect their already dicey driving. What we're seeing now is an unfortunate and predictable outcome. It's a cash and carry business. With more small-time dealers operating turf encroachment is inevitable. This tends to make drug dealers angry." Wellesly Deputy Police Chief William Brooks III, speaking on behalf of the Massachusetts Chiefs of Police Association said "the whole thing is a mess. The perception out there among a lot of people is it's ok to do it now, so there's an uptick in

the number of people wanting to do it...Most of the drug-related
violence you see now – the shootings, murders – is about weed."
Several 2010 high-profile killings have been linked by law
enforcement to the increased market:

- The May fatal shooting of a 21-year-old inside a Harvard
  University dorm, allegedly in a bid to rob him of his pot and cash.
- The June murder of a 17-year-old in Callahan State Park, where
  he was lured by two men seeking revenge in a fight over
  marijuana.
- The September massacre of four people in Mattapan, including a
  21-year-old woman and her 2-year-old son, over an alleged pot-
  dealing turf dispute.
- The September fatal shooting of a 29-year-old man, by four men,
  one a high school senior, in connection with robbery and murder
  of a drug dealer.[225]

- Children often bear the consequences of actions engaged in by parents
  or guardians involved with marijuana.
  - In Bradenton, Florida a Highway Patrol officer tried to stop a man
    speeding on I-75. The driver did not stop until he ran up on the
    median and crashed into a construction barrel. In the car the
    troopers found three small children, forty pounds of marijuana
    and several thousand dollars in cash.[226]
  - A Hamilton, Montana man put his three toddlers in the back seat
    of his one ton Chevy pickup and then partied with a friend as he
    drove along the highway. At 50 miles an hour he swerved into
    another car killing the owner. While partying with his friend in
    the vehicle he had smoked two bowls of pot.[227]
  - An Ohio mother is accused of teaching her two-year-old daughter
    smoke pot and recording the incident on her cell phone.[228]
  - A Virginia mother and her roommate were charged with reckless
    child endangerment after her two-year-old daughter ingested an
    unknown amount of marijuana in a motel room.[229]
  - A California couple was arrested after a video surfaced of them
    allowing their 23-month-old son to use a marijuana pipe. The
    video showed the child smoking the pipe. The pipe was tested and
    found to have marijuana residue in it. Both parents said they had
    medical marijuana cards, but could not explain why they would
    give it to their child and then videotape the incident.[230]

- Cincinnati, Ohio police arrested a woman for allegedly giving her three children, ages seven, four and one marijuana. The seven-year-old told the school counselor that she had been forced to smoke marijuana. All three children tested positive for marijuana.[231]
- In Stockton, California a two-year-old girl was in critical condition after ingesting marijuana resin. Although four adults were home at the time, none were supervising the child when she found a jar lid containing resin.[232]
- Two toddlers in Louisiana were hospitalized after ingesting marijuana and amphetamines. A search warrant of the home found several unsecured bottles of prescription medication and a hand-rolled cigar containing marijuana.[233]
- In Santa Clara, California, in one week in December, four dispensaries and one marijuana grower were hit by vandals, burglars, or armed robbers. At one location four suspects robbed the victim by throwing him to the floor, holding a piece of metal to his throat, and demanding marijuana and money. At one dispensary, the owner, who is paralyzed and in a wheelchair, was closing up the shop when armed robbers knocked him over and barged in. The robbers tied him up and took marijuana and cash.[234]
- The Los Angeles Police Department is investigating a series of robberies and shootings at marijuana dispensaries. Over a one week period in June 2010 a Northridge dispensary robbery left one employee in critical condition after being shot in the face; the shooting was the second at that business that year and the third dispensary to be targeted in three days. Two people were fatally shot in a pot shop robberies in Echo Park and Hollywood, and a third person was wounded.[235]
- On March 4, 2010, a California man was killed after opening fire on two Pentagon Police Officers. In a story on MSNBC, the Friday before the incident, John Patrick Bedell's parents had warned local authorities that his behavior had become erratic and that he was unstable and had a gun. Bedell was diagnosed as bipolar and had been in and out of treatment programs for years. His psychiatrist, J. Michael Nelson, said "Bedell tried to self-medicate with marijuana, inadvertently making his symptoms more pronounced."[236] Bedell had been given a prescription for medical use of marijuana in 2006 for chronic insomnia. According to long-time friend Reb Monaco "he

was not a person who should have been issued a medical clearance to use marijuana, but he was."[237]

- A marijuana dealer kidnapped and murdered a 15 year-old boy after he got angry at the teen's half-brother for owing him a $2,500 drug debt.[238]

- A 27-year-old lawyer, Oxford educated, fell to his death from the top floor of a London building following years of treatment for cannabis-induced mental illness. The February 2007 inquest revealed that he had been suffering from bi-polar affective disorder-manic depression, which "may have been triggered by cannabis use."[239]

- Marijuana also creates hazards that are not always predictable. In August 2004, two Philadelphia firefighters died battling a fire that started because of tangled wires and lamps used to grow marijuana in a basement closet.[240]

- All six people aboard a Piper Cherokee were killed when it crashed soon after take-off on Hamilton Island in North Queensland, Australia on September 2002. Toxicologist Professor Olaf Drummer told the inquest that blood tests on the 27-year-old pilot indicated that he had used marijuana either in the hours leading up to the crash or he could have been a regular user.[241]

- Grant Everson and three friends armed with box cutters and a shotgun slipped into Everson's parents' Chaska, Minnesota home demanding money to open a coffeehouse in the marijuana-friendly City of Amsterdam. Although Grant lost his nerve, his friends proceeded to shoot and kill his mother.
All four were arrested. Their alibi was that they had been sleeping in the same Burnsville apartment after a night of smoking marijuana and playing video games.[242]

- The National Transportation Safety Board investigation of a small plane crash near Walnut Ridge, Arkansas, killing a passenger and the pilot, was a result of pilot error.
Pilot Jason Heard failed to fly high enough and maintain enough airspeed to avoid a stall. The report notes that Pilot Jason Heard had enough marijuana in his system to have contributed to the accident.[243]

Marijuana and Incarceration

Federal marijuana investigations and prosecutions usually involve hundreds of pounds of marijuana. Few defendants are incarcerated in federal prison for simple possession of marijuana.

- In 2008, according to the United States Sentencing Commission (USSC), 25,337 people were sentenced in federal court for drug crimes under six offense categories. Marijuana accounted for 6,337 (25 percent). Looking even further, of the 6, 337 people sentenced, only 99 people or 1.6 percent, were sentenced for "simple possession" of marijuana.[244]
- According to a Bureau of Justice Statistics survey of state and federal prisoners published in October 2006, approximately 12.7 percent of state prisoners and 12.4 percent of federal prisoners were serving time for a marijuana-related offense. This is a decrease from 1997 when these figures were 12.9 percent and 18.9 percent respectively.[245]
- Between October 1, 2005 and September 30, 2006, there were 6,423 federal offenders sentenced for marijuana-related charges in the U.S. Courts. Approximately 95.9 percent of the cases involved trafficking.[246]
- In Fiscal Year 2006, there were 25,814 offenders sentenced in federal court on drug charges. Of those, only 1.6 percent (406 people) were sentenced for simple possession.[247]
- According to the White House Office of National Drug Control Policy, "Many inmates ultimately sentenced for marijuana and possession were initially charged with more serious crimes but were able to negotiate reduced charges or lighter sentences through plea agreements with prosecutors. Therefore the ...figure for simple possession defendants may give an inflated impression of the true numbers, since it also includes these inmates who pled down from more serious charges." [248]
- Findings from the 2008 Arrestee Drug Abuse Monitoring System (ADAM II), which surveys drug use among booked male arrestees in ten major metropolitan areas across the country, shows the majority of arrestees in each city test positive for illicit drug use, with as many as 87 percent of arrestees testing positive for an illegal drug. Marijuana is the most commonly detected drug at the time of the arrest. In seven

of the ten sites arrestees who are using marijuana are using it on the average of every other day for the past 30 days.[249]

The Foreign Experience with Marijuana

Many European countries are re-thinking their liberal marijuana policies in the face of evidence that cannabis use has significant mental and physical consequences and may lead to higher crime rates, increased social costs and degradation of their quality of life. "Few adults in Europe believe marijuana should be readily available for personal consumption," according to the Eurobarometer conducted by NS Opinion and Social in September -October, 2006. "Only 26 percent of respondents in 30 countries believe cannabis should be legalized."[250]

There is no uniform drug policy in Europe. Some countries have liberalized their laws, while others have instituted strict drug control policies, which mean that the so called "European Model" is a misnomer. Like America, the various countries of Europe are looking for new ways to combat the worldwide problem of drug abuse.

In recent years the European Monitoring Center for Drugs and Drug Addiction (EMCDDA) has reported a tendency among European countries to make a stronger distinction between those who use drugs and those who sell or traffic drugs. This distinction is reflected in the reduction of penalties for drug use in some countries, though others have not changed or increased penalties. EMCDDA reports that recently, the penalties for drug offenses in Europe have generally increased. "Most of the reported drug law offenses are related to use and possession for use rather than supply, and whereas offenses related to supply increased by 12 percent, those related to possession have increased by over 50 percent." Cannabis continued to be the drug most often associated with drug law offenses. The view expressed by some that in Europe you are unlikely to be charged with a drug offense if caught using marijuana is not supported by the data.[251]

In the Annual Report for 2010, the EMCDDA has noted the increase in domestic cannabis production and its resulting negative effects. According to Wolfgang Götz, "Organized crime gangs have woken up to the profits that can accrue from the large-scale cultivation of cannabis near its intended market. The collateral damage of this development is the rising level of violence and criminality within urban communities, which is now triggering new action by the national and European law-enforcement bodies."[252]

Australia

- On October 11, 2009 Premier Colin Barnett announced that the Government "would introduce legislation to repeal the Cannabis Control Act 2003 and make changes to the Misuse of Drugs Act 1981 and the Young Offenders Act 1994, sending a clear message that the current State Government did not endorse illicit drug use." "The new anti-cannabis laws will mark the start of the Liberal-National Government's fight to turn around eight years of a soft-on-drugs approach by the previous Labor government which has left lives ruined."[253]
- In a reversal of their 2006 official position, the Australian Medical Association has called on the state government of Western Australia to introduce harsher marijuana laws. The AMA cited a recent review of international research on the links between marijuana and mental illness. AMA president Dr. Rosanna Capolingua said that "soft marijuana laws certainly do not help support the message that marijuana is not a soft drug."[254]
- Drug Free Australia official Craig Thompson is urging the community, young people in particular, to change their thinking about cannabis because of its serious effects on health. "The road fatalities caused by cannabis-intoxicated drivers, links to cannabis and psychosis, birth defects and greater potency of the drug are just a few issues of enormous concern," Mr. Thompson said.[255]

Canada

- In August 2006, Ontario gave new powers to police, utilities and municipalities to crack down on marijuana grow operations and methamphetamine labs running from residential locations. The province's anti-drug legislation was toughened to protect communities and allows police to work more effectively with citizens in identifying and uprooting marijuana operations. New provisions to the law include allowing water and power utilities officials to inspect buildings suspected to house marijuana grow operations.[256]
- After a large decline in the 1980s, marijuana use among teens increased during the 1990s as young people became "confused about the state of federal pot law" in the wake of an aggressive decriminalization campaign, according to a special adviser to Health Canada's Director General of Drug Strategy. Several Canadian drug surveys show that marijuana use among Canadian youth has steadily

climbed to surpass its 26-year peak, rising to 29.6 percent of youth in grades 7-12 in 2003.[257]

Germany

- As The Netherlands cracks down on cannabis cultivation, it is pushing its drug gangs into Germany. Since 2004, 30 "cannabis plantations" have been shut down near the Dutch border. In addition, the Dutch government has forced a number of "coffee shops" that sell illegally produced hash and marijuana to move their operations out of city centers and closer to the Dutch-German border. Demand for marijuana among German youth is higher than ever, and investigators in Krefeld estimate that the coffee shops attract 54,000 customers each month, with 50,000 coming from Germany.[258]

The Netherlands

- The Netherlands has led Europe in the liberalization of drug policy. "Coffee shops" began to emerge throughout The Netherlands in 1976, offering marijuana products for sale. Possession and sale of marijuana are not legal, but coffee shops are permitted to operate and sell marijuana under certain restrictions, including a limit of no more than 5 grams sold to a person at any one time, no alcohol or hard drugs, no minors, and no advertising. In The Netherlands it is illegal to sell or possess marijuana products. So coffee shop operators must purchase their marijuana products from illegal drug trafficking organizations.
- On January 2, 2007, the majority of the City Council in Amsterdam voted in favor of introducing a city-wide ban on smoking marijuana in public in areas where young people smoking joints have been causing a public nuisance. Their decision was based upon the success of the experimental ban in DeBaarsjes.[259]
- According to a *New York Times* article, "The mayor (of Maastricht) wants to move most of the city's 16 licensed cannabis clubs to the edge of town, preferably close to the border" (with Belgium and Germany). Mayor Gerd Leers is reacting to growing concerns among residents who "complain of traffic problems, petty crime, loitering and public urination. There have been shootings between Balkan gangs. Maastricht's small police force...is already spending one-third of its time on drug-related problems." Cannabis clubs have drawn "pushers of hard drugs from Amsterdam, who often harass people on the streets." The clubs have also attracted people looking to buy

marijuana in quantity. Piet Tans, the police spokesman also stated that "People who come from far away don't just come for the five grams you can buy legally over the counter...They think pounds and kilos; they go to the dealers who operate in the shadows."[260]

- Moving the clubs did not prove to be an effective strategy to deal with the problem. As of January 1, 2010, coffee shops in the province of Limburg (which includes Maastricht) will be accessible only to registered members. Justice Minister Ernst Hirsch Ballin also stated that "it would become easier to keep minors out of the coffee shops."[261]

- Although the Dutch government regulated what goes on in coffee shops, they have never legalized or regulated how the shops got their marijuana supply. The volume of sales generated by customers from bordering countries and tourists have made these shops regional suppliers. This has resulted in the creation of an illegal cultivation industry involving organized crime and money laundering.

- Paul Schnabel, director for the Social and Cultural Planning Office, a government advisory board, said that the move reflects a growing view that the tolerance policies have not controlled the ills associated with drugs and prostitution. "There's a strong tendency in Dutch society to control things by allowing them..." "Dutch society is less willing to tolerate than before."[262]

- Due to international pressure on permissive Dutch cannabis policy and domestic complaints over the spread of marijuana "coffee shops," the Government of the Netherlands has reconsidered its legalization measures. After marijuana became normalized, consumption nearly tripled – from 15 percent to 44 percent – among 18 to 20 year-old Dutch youth.[263] As a result of stricter local government policies, the number of cannabis "coffeehouses" in the Netherlands was reduced – from 1,179 in 1997[264] to 737 in 2004, a 37 percent decrease in 7 years.[265]

- About 70 percent of Dutch towns have a zero-tolerance policy toward cannabis cafes.[266]

- Dr. Ernest Bunning, formerly with Holland's Ministry of Health and a principal proponent of that country's liberal drug philosophy, has acknowledged that, "[t]here are young people who abuse soft drugs . . . particularly those that have [a] high THC [content]. The place that cannabis takes in their lives becomes so dominant they don't have space for the other important things in life. They crawl out of bed in the morning, grab a joint, don't work, smoke another joint. They don't know what to do with their lives."[267]

- "Contrary to what is often claimed by supporters of the Dutch drug policy, cannabis usage by young people in The Netherlands is not lower but actually higher than average in Europe," according to the findings of the 2007 European School Survey on Alcohol and Other Drugs (ESPAD). "The Netherlands scores above the European average. Over one-quarter (28 percent) of the youngsters aged 15 and 16 surveyed said they have used cannabis sometime in their life, compared with an average of 19 percent in Europe. Current Cannabis usage (at least once in the month prior to the survey) is more than double the European average in The Netherlands (15 percent versus 7 percent)."[268]

- An article published in April 2009 summarizes the challenge now faced by the Dutch as a result of their drug policies. "The Netherlands has risen in the ranking order of 35 European countries from number 12 in 2003 to number 5 on recent cannabis usage...The Dutch youngsters, possibly due to the liberal climate, widely believe that cannabis is innocent. The proportion of school children that thinks regular cannabis usage involves big risks is the lowest in the Netherlands (50 percent) of all countries surveyed."[269]

Portugal

- In July 2001, Portugal decriminalized all drugs, increased drug education efforts, and expanded the drug treatment programs. Drug possession for personal use and drug usage are still legally prohibited, although treated through an administrative process rather than a criminal one. Instead of being placed in the judicial system they are sent to dissuasion commissions run by the government. The commissions, made up of doctors, lawyers, and social workers, encourage addicts to undergo treatment and stop recreational users from becoming addicts.

- Anyone having enough drugs to exceed a ten day supply can be arrested, sentenced to jail, or given a criminal record. Drug trafficking is still a criminal offense.

- There is still much debate upon the success of this initiative. Those on each side of the legalization debate argue as to whether or not things improved in Portugal as a result of the decriminalization of use or as a result of the prevention efforts and accessibility of treatment programs. There are many different views on the measurement of the successes or failures of this initiative. Would the same results have happened if Portugal offered the emphasis of drug education and the accessibility of drug treatment without decriminalizing drug use? Would treating drug use and addiction as a health problem rather than a criminal justice problem have produced similar results?

- Clearly there is still plenty of work that needs to be done. The latest EMCDDA report reveals that drug use among the general population is still rising. The number of Portuguese aged 15 to 64 who have ever tried drugs has climbed from 7.8 percent in 2001 to 12 percent in 2007. Cannabis use went up from 7.6 percent to 11.7 percent.[270]

- What is clear is that Portugal believes that it is a combination of prevention, education, treatment and law enforcement that is needed to address the drug situation – no one aspect alone can effectively eradicate drug use and the problems it causes. This is the same strategy that is used by the United States.

Singapore

- As of August 1, 2007, marijuana users caught in Singapore face mandatory treatment in Drug Rehabilitation Centers. However, people who undergo the treatment and subsequently get arrested again for marijuana use face a mandatory minimum five-year prison sentence, plus three strokes of the cane. Three-time offenders get seven years in prison plus six strokes.[271]

Switzerland

- In December 2008, 63 percent of Swiss voters voted against an initiative to decriminalize marijuana. The government, which opposed the proposal, feared that liberalizing marijuana would cause problems from neighboring countries. "This could lead to a situation where you have some sort of cannabis tourism in Switzerland because of something that is illegal in the EU would be legal in Switzerland," a government spokesman said.[272]

- Liberalization of marijuana laws in Switzerland has likewise produced damaging results. After liberalization, Switzerland became a magnet for drug users from many other countries. In 1987, Zurich permitted drug use and sales in a part of the city called Platzpitz, dubbed "Needle Park." By 1992, the number of regular drug users at the park reportedly swelled from a "few hundred at the outset in 1987 to about

20,000." The area around the park became crime-ridden, forcing closure of the park. The experiment has since been terminated.[273]

United Kingdom

- A 2009 Scottish Social Attitudes Survey on public attitudes toward illegal drugs and misuse in Scotland found a reversal in the tolerant attitudes toward cannabis. Support for legalization fell from 37 percent in 2001 to 24 percent in 2009. Even among those that had tried cannabis, support for legalization fell from 70 percent in 2001 to 47 percent in 2009. Attitudes for prosecution for possession hardened during the same time period. In 2001, 51 percent felt that people should not be prosecuted for possession of a small amount of cannabis for personal use, but in 2009 only 34 percent concurred. Most startling was the fact that the shifts were most prevalent among 18-24 year-olds. In 2001 62 percent of this age group was in favor of legalization; in 2009, only 24 percent felt that way.[274]

- In a statement to the press, Home Secretary Jacqui Smith announced on May 8, 2008 that cannabis is being reclassified back to a Class B drug, sending a strong message that the drug is harmful. Addressing the House of Commons, Secretary Smith cited the need to update public policies to match recent scientific evidence about the serious harms of marijuana use; "the enforcement response must reflect the danger that the drug poses to individuals, and in turn, to communities."[275]

- A major newspaper in England, *The Independent on Sunday,* reversed its very public stance in support of marijuana. After a pro-cannabis editorial appeared in 1997, 16,000 people marched on London's Hyde Park. The editorial and the subsequent march were credited with forcing the government to downgrade the legal status of cannabis to class C. However, an editorial in the March 18, 2007 issue, titled "Cannabis: An Apology," states that the paper is reversing its decision. "In 1997, when this paper called for decriminalization, 1,600 people were being treated for cannabis addiction. Today, the number is 22,000." Concerns such as the record number of teenagers requiring drug treatment as a result of smoking skunk (a highly potent cannabis strain) and the growing proof that skunk causes mental illness were cited among the reasons for this reversal.[276]

- In March 2005, British Home Secretary Charles Clarke took the unprecedented step of calling "for a rethink on Labour's legal downgrading of cannabis" from a Class B to a Class C substance. Mr. Clarke requested that the Advisory Council on the Misuse of Drugs complete a new report, taking into account recent studies showing a link between cannabis and psychosis and also considering the more potent cannabis referred to as "skunk."[277]

- In 2005, during a general election speech to concerned parents, British Prime Minister Tony Blair noted that medical evidence increasingly suggests that cannabis is not as harmless as people think and warned parents that young people who smoke cannabis could move on to harder drugs.[278]

2006 World Drug Report

- The *2006 World Drug Report* outlines significant global progress achieved in reducing the threat of drugs over 2005 and also highlights challenges to international efforts to stem the trafficking, use and production of dangerous, addictive drugs. Among the key findings of this report is that drug traffickers have invested heavily in increasing the potency of cannabis, which has produced devastating effects. As a result, the characteristics of cannabis are no longer that different from those of other plant-based drugs, such as cocaine and heroin. This report contends that differing messages as well as legislative changes by various governments regarding marijuana leave young people confused as to just how dangerous cannabis is.[279]

OTHER CONSIDERATIONS

Marijuana Use among Youth Is Rising as Perception of Risk Decreases

- In December 2010, the Monitoring the Future Report indicated that after watching marijuana use have a gradual and steady decline in the last decade this trend has changed.
- Marijuana use rose for all prevalence periods this year – lifetime, past year, past 30-days, and daily in the past 30-days – for all three grades.
- Daily or near-daily use of marijuana (use on 20 or more occasions in the prior 30 days) increased significantly: for 8th (1.2 percent), 10th

(3.3 percent) and 12th (6.1 percent) graders. This means that for 12th graders one in sixteen use marijuana on a daily or near-daily basis.

- One possible explanation for the resurgence in marijuana use is that in recent years fewer teens report seeing much danger associated with its use, even regular use. Both perceived risk and disapproval continued to decline in all three grades this year.[280]

- The perception that regular marijuana smoking is harmful decreased for 10th graders (down from 59.4 percent in 2009 to 57.2 percent in 2010) and 12th graders (from 52.4 percent in 2009 to 46.8 percent in 2010). Moreover disapproval of smoking marijuana decreased significantly among 8th graders.

- For 12th graders, declines in cigarette use accompanied by recent increase in marijuana use have put marijuana ahead of cigarette smoking in some measures. In 2010, 21.4 percent of high school seniors used marijuana in the past 30 days, while 19.2 percent smoked cigarettes.

- "We should examine the extent to which the debate over medical marijuana and marijuana legalization for adults is affecting teens' perceptions of risk," said NIDA Director Dr. Nora Volkow. We must also find better ways to communicate to teens that marijuana use can harm their short-term performance as well as their long-term potential."[281]

- The 2009 National Survey on Drug Use and Health shows that among youth aged 12 to 17, the current illicit drug use rate increased from 2008 (9.3 percent) to 2009 (10 percent) and increased for marijuana use from 6.7 percent to 7.3 percent.[282]

- The percentage of youths aged 12 to 17 indicating great risk in smoking marijuana once a month decreased from 33.9 percent in 2008 to 30.7 percent in 2009.[283]

- The rate of youths aged 12 to 17 perceiving great risk in smoking marijuana once or twice a week also decreased from 33.9 percent in 2008 to 30.7 percent in 2009.[284]

- The 2009 Partnership Attitude Tracking Study (PATS), an annual survey of teens in grades 9 through 12 also shows a reversal in the declines in teen abuse and alcohol that hasn't been seen since 1998. Past year use of marijuana shows a 19 percent increase (from 32 percent in 2008 to 38 percent in 2009). Between 1998-2008 marijuana use had decreased by 30 percent. Underlying these increases are negative shifts in teen attitudes, particularly a growing belief in the benefits and acceptability of drug use and drinking.[285]

Increased Eradication

- During 2009, DEA's Domestic Cannabis Eradication/Suppression Program supported the eradication of 9,474,867 plants in the top seven marijuana producing states (California, Kentucky, Oregon, Tennessee, Utah, Washington, and West Virginia). This is an increase of 2,325,335 eradicated plants over the previous year.[286]
- During the 2009 eradication season, a total of over 10.3 million marijuana plants were eradicated across the United States. This is a 2.38 million plant increase over 2008.[287]

In Their Own Words

"We created Prop. 215 so patients would not have to deal with the black market profiteers. But today it is all about the money. Most of the dispensaries operating in California are a little more than dope dealers with store fronts."

- **Reverend Scott T. Imler**, co-author of Proposition 215, the 1996 ballot initiative that legalized medical marijuana in California, Alternatives Magazine, Fall 2006, issue 39.

"When we wrote Proposition 215, we were selling it to the public as something for seriously ill people... It's turned into a joke. I think a lot of people have medicalized their recreational use."

- **Reverend Scott T. Imler,** in an interview with Sandy Mazza, *San Gabriel Valley Tribune*, February 15, 2007.

"No reasonable person would have gathered that they were voting on setting up marijuana stores back in 1996."

- **Mark A.R. Kleinman**, Professor of Public Policy, UCLA, December 27, 2006.

"Quitting cannabis has been an important part of my recovery from mental illness. Marijuana can trigger psychosis. Every time I was hospitalized it was preceded by heavy marijuana use."

- **Margaret Trudeau**, ex-wife of former Canadian Prime Minister Pierre Trudeau, at the Canadian Mental Health Conference in Vancouver, February 15, 2007.

"Many [people] subscribe to the vague, laissez-faire tolerance of cannabis which is increasingly prevalent among educated people in Western countries. That consensus needs to be challenged. Evidence of the damage to mental health caused by cannabis use is mounting and cannot be ignored." "It is time to explode the myth of cannabis as a "soft" drug."

- **Antonio Maria Costa**, Executive Director, United Nations Office on Drugs and Crime, March 2007.

"Traditional 1960s herbal cannabis contained about 2-3 percent of the active ingredient tetrahydrocannabinol (THC); but today's skunk varieties may contain 15 or 20 percent THC, and new resin preparations have up to 30 percent. Skunk is to old-fashioned hash as whiskey is to lager. You can become an alcoholic just by drinking lager; but you have to drink a lot more lager than whiskey. Similarly, you can go psychotic if you smoke enough traditional marijuana, but you have to consume a lot more for a longer time than with skunk."

- **Professor Robin Murray**, London's Institute of Psychiatry, *The Independent on Sunday*, March 21, 2007.

"I've been astonished by the way medical marijuana has become a commercial business... The energy is in medical marijuana for the younger generation, and there's an actual economy of it."

- **Dale Gieringer**, Director of California NORML and a Proposition 215 author, in an interview with Vanessa Grigoriadis, *Rolling Stone* magazine, February 7, 2007.

"Our current experience with legal, regulated prescription drugs like Oxycontin shows that legalizing drugs in not a panacea. In fact, its legalization widens its availability and misuse, no matter what controls are in place."

- **Gil Kerlikowske**, Director, ONDCP, *Why Marijuana Legalization Would Compromise Public Health and Safety*, Annotated Remarks to the California Police Chiefs Association Conference, March 4, 2010.

APPENDIX. ACRONYMS USED IN "THE DEA POSITION ON MARIJUANA"

AAP	American Academy of Pediatrics
ACS	American Cancer Society
ADAM	Arrestee Drug and Alcohol Monitoring
AMA	American Medical Association
BBC	British Broadcasting Company
BMA	British Medical Association
CADCA	Community Anti-Drug Coalitions of America
CB1	Cannabinoid Receptor 1: one of two receptors in the brain's endocannabinoid (EC) system associated with the intake of food and tobacco dependency.
CBD	Cannabidiol, one of the cannabinoids found in marijuana
CMCR	Center for Medicinal Cannabis Research
DASIS	Drug and Alcohol Services Information System
DEA	Drug Enforcement Administration
EMCDDA	European Monitoring Center for Drugs and Drug Addiction
FDA	Food and Drug Administration
HIV	Human Immunodeficiency Virus
INCB	International Narcotics Control Board
IOM	Institute of Medicine
IOP	Intraocular Pressure
LSD	Diethylamide-Lysergic Acid
MS	Multiple Sclerosis
MTF	*Monitoring the Future,* an annual survey conducted by the University of Michigan on youth drug use
NHTSA	National Highway Traffic Safety Administration
NIDA	National Institute on Drug Abuse

NMSS   National Multiple Sclerosis Society
NORML   National Organization for the Reform of Marijuana Laws
NSDUH   National Survey of Drug Use and Health
ONDCP   Office of National Drug Control Policy
TEDS   Treatment Episode Data Set
THC   Tetrahydrocannabinol, the main psychoactive substance
           found in the marijuana plant
USSC   United States Sentencing Commission

End Notes

[1] As of December 31, 2010, the 15 states that have decriminalized certain marijuana use are Alaska, Arizona, California, Colorado, Hawaii, Maine, Michigan, Montana, Nevada, New Jersey, New Mexico, Oregon, Rhode Island, Vermont, and Washington. In addition, Maryland has enacted legislation that recognizes a "medical marijuana" defense and Massachusetts replaced criminal penalties for adult possession of less than one ounce of marijuana with civil penalties. In Washington D.C. the Legalization of Marijuana for Medical Treatment Amendment Act of 2010 became law in July 2011.

[2] Memorandum from Deputy Attorney General David W. Ogden to the United States Attorneys, "Investigations and Prosecutions in States Authorizing the Medical Use of Marijuana." October 19, 2009 and Department of Justice Press Release 09-1119, October 19, 2009.

[3] "Inter-Agency Advisory Regarding Claims That Smoked Marijuana Is a Medicine." *U.S. Food and Drug Administration*, April 20, 2006. <http://www.fda.gov/NewsEvents/Newsroom/PressAnnouncements/2006/ucm/108643.htm>.

[4] "INCB: US Supreme Court Decision on Cannabis Upholds International Law." Professor Hamid Ghodse, President of the INCB. Press Release. June 8, 2005.

[5] "Policy H-95.952 'Medical Marijuana.'" American Medical Association, Report 3 of the Council on Science and Public Health (I-09) Use of Cannabis for Medicinal Purposes.

[6] ASAM Public Policy on "Medical Marijuana." (April 23, 2010) http://www.wfad.se/latest-news/1-articles/213-asam-public-policy-statement-on-qmedical-marijuanaq.

[7] "Experts: Pot Smoking Is Not Best Choice to Treat Chemo Side-Effects." *American Cancer Society.* May 22, 2001. http://www.cancer.org/docroot/NWS/content/update/NWS_1_1xU_Experts_Pot_Smoking_Is_Not_Best_Choice_to_Treat_Chemo_Side_Effects.asp> (March 9, 2005).

[8] "American Glaucoma Society Position Statement: Marijuana and the Treatment of Glaucoma." Jampel, Henry MD. MHS, Journal of Glaucoma: February 2010-Volume 19-Issue 2 –pp.75-76 doi:10.1097/IJG.obo13e3181d12e39. also www.glaucomaweb.org.

[9] Committee on Substance Abuse and Committee on Adolescence. "Legalization of Marijuana: Potential Impact on Youth." *Pediatrics* Vol. 113, No. 6 (June 6, 2004): 1825-1826. *See also,* Joffe, Alain, MD, MPH, and Yancy, Samuel, MD. "Legalization of Marijuana: Potential Impact on Youth." *Pediatrics* Vol. 113, No. 6 (June 6, 2004): e632-e638h.

[10] "Recommendations Regarding the Use of Cannabis in Multiple Sclerosis: Executive Summary." *National Clinical Advisory Board of the National Multiple Sclerosis Society*, Expert Opinion Paper, Treatment Recommendations for Physicians, April 2, 2008. http://www.nationalmssociety.org.

[11] "Doctors' Fears at Cannabis Change." *BBC News.* January 21, 2004.

[12] *Manchester Online.* "Doctors Support Drive Against Cannabis." *Manchester News.* January 21, 2004.   <http://www.manchesteronline.co.uk/news/s/78/78826_doctors_support_drive_against_cannabis.html> (March 25, 2005).
[13] *Institute of Medicine.* "Marijuana and Medicine: Assessing the Science Base." (1999). Summary. <http://www.nap.edu/html/marimed> (April 12, 2005).
[14] Id.
[15] *Institute of Medicine.* "Marijuana and Medicine: Assessing the Science Base." (1999). Executive Summary. <http://www.nap.edu/html/marimed> (January 11, 2006).
[16] *Institute of Medicine.* "Marijuana and Medicine: Assessing the Science Base." (1999). Summary. <http://www.nap.edu/html/marimed> (January 11, 2006).
[17] *Institute of Medicine.* "Marijuana and Medicine: Assessing the Science Base." (1999). Summary. <http://www.nap.edu/html/marimed> (January 11, 2006).
[18] Benson, John A., Jr. and Watson, Stanley J., Jr. "Strike a Balance in the Marijuana Debate." *The Standard-Times.* 13 April 1999.
[19] DEA, Office of Diversion Control, December 28, 2010.
[20] GW Announces UK Launch of World's First Prescription Medicine, Press Release, June 21, 2010. http://www.gwpharma.com/release-sativex-launch.aspx. see also "The Development of Modern Cannabis-Based Medications: Myth and Facts." PowerPoint presentation to the 2010 Oregon Summit: The Impact of Marijuana, April 27, 2010, Mead, Alice, Director, U.S. Professional Relations, GW Pharmaceuticals.
[21] Stannard, Matthew B. "Ecstasy Victim Told Friends She Felt Like She Was Going to Die." *The San Francisco Chronicle,* May 4, 2004. The Chronicle reported that Ms. Perez was given ibuprofen and "possibly marijuana," but the DEA has confirmed that the drug given to her was indeed marijuana.
[22] Marijuana Policy Project's Vision and Mission Statement. *www.mpp.org.*
[23] From a videotape recording of Mr. Rosenthal's speech, as shown in "Medical Marijuana: A Smoke Screen."
[24] "A Guide to Drug Related State Ballot Initiatives." *National Families in Action.* April 23, 2002. <http://www.nationalfamilies.org/guide/california215.html> (March 31, 2005).
[25] Wren, Christopher S. "Small But Forceful Coalition Works to Counter U.S. War on Drugs." *The New York Times,* January 2, 2000.
[26] Craig, Tim. "Md. Starts to Allow Marijuana Court Plea; Penalty Can be Cut for Medicinal Use." *The Washington Post.* October 1, 2003, sec B.
[27] Brant, Tataboline. "Marijuana Campaign Draws in $857,000." *The Anchorage Daily News.* October 30, 2004.
[28] Gathright, Alan. "Pot Backers Can't Stoke Hickenlooper." *Rocky Mountain News.* October 27, 2005.
[29] Marijuana Initiatives: November 2006. *Marijuana Policy Project. www.mpp.org.*
[30] Ibid.
[31] Ibid.
[32] "Court Action Filed by Hailey City Officials on Voter Adopted Marijuana and Hemp Ordinances." Hailey City Hall Press Release, May 13, 2008. http://www.haileycityhall.org/news_event/news/2008/MarijuanaCourtActionPressRelease.pdf.
[33] "Hailey changes course on pot initiatives: Council decides to litigate rather than amend policies." Idaho Mountain Express. January 30, 2008. http:www.mtexpres.com/index2.php?ID=2005119141.
[34] "Judge Neuters Hailey Pot Initiatives." Terry Smith, Idaho Mountain Express, March 27, 2009. http://www.mtexpress.com/index2.php?ID=2005125415.
[35] 2008 Ballot Initiatives, Marijuana Policy Project, http://www.mpp.org/library/2008-ballot-initiatives.html.
[36] Ibid.
[37] Ibid.
[38] Ibid.

[39] Ibid.

[40] "Medical Marijuana Bill Vetoed." Karen Langley, Concord Monitor, July 13, 2009. http://www.concordmonitor.com/apps/pbcs.dll/article?AID=/20090711/FRONTPAGE/907110312/1001/NEWS01.

[41] "RI Assembly overrides veto on marijuana compassion centers." Donita Naylor and Cynthia Needham, the Providence Journal, June 17, 2009.

[42] "Medical marijuana grower to begin distribution." Jeremy Jojola and Matthew Kappus, June 3, 2009. http://www.kob.com/article/stories/5961683.shtml.

[43] "Medical Marijuana Expansion Approved by a Wide Margin." Meg Haskell, MPBN, Maine Public Broadcasting Network, November 4, 2009. http://www.mpbn.net/Home/tabid/36/ctl/ViewItem/mid/3478/ZItemId/9642/Default.aspx.

[44] "Colorado Town Will Decriminalize Possession as Medical Marijuana Movement Gains Steam." CBS news, November 4, 2009.

[45] "N.J. Medical Marijuana Law Overlooks Many In Pain." Susan Donaldson James, January 18, 2010, http://www.abcnews.go.com/Health/wellness/nj-medical-marijuana-law-ignores-chronic-pain-sufferers/story?id=95744509.

[46] "N.J. Medical Marijuana Law Deadline to be Delayed to Next Year." http://www.nj.com/news/index.ssf/2010/06/nj_medical_marijuana_law_could.html.

[47] " Marijuana Questions on Some Massachusetts Ballots." Phillip Smith. September 29, 2010. Http://stopthedrugwar.org/chronicle/2010/sep/29/marijuana_questions_some_massach. "The Victories That Got Overlooked – and Still Lie Ahead." Rob Kampia. November 4, 2010. http://www.huffingtonpost.com/rob-kampia/the-mj-victoriies-t-_b_778945.html.

[48] "Arizona voters approve medical marijuana measure." http://www.cbsnews.com/storeis/2010/11/12/national/main/7052327.html. Mark deBernardo "Arizona Passes 'Medical-Marijuana' Initiative," Legislative Update. Institute for a Drug-Free Workplace. November 17, 2010.

[49] 'South Dakota voters say no to medical marijuana." Lynn Taylor Rick. Rapid City Journal. November 3, 2010. http://www.rapidcityjournal.com/news/article_1ae826c6-e6f2-11df-8018-001cc4c002eo.html.

[50] "Oregon Voters See Folly in Expanding Medi-Pot Program." Press Release. S.O.S. and the Drug Free American Foundation, Inc. November 2, 2010. http://www.saveoursociety.org/issues-leglislation-o.

[51] "Measure to Legalize Marijuana Loses in California." AOL news. November 3, 2010. http://www.aolnews.com/2010/11/03/california-voters-reject-legalization-of-marijuana/.

[52] This Year's Top 10 Domestic Drug Policy Stories." Phillip Smith. Drug War Chronicles, Issue #664. December 22, 2010. http://stopthedrugwar.org/chronicle/2010/dec/22/years_top_10_domestic_drug_polic.

[53] Press Statement of Former DEA of Former DEA Administrators Robert C. Bonner and Peter Bensinger. October 15, 2010. http://www.theiacp.org/About/PressCenter/MarijuanaLegalizationIssue/tabid/756/Default.aspx

[54] Ibid.

[55] "CQ Floor Votes." Congressional Quarterly, Inc. July 25, 2007. www.nctimes.com/artoc;es/2005/11/02/news/top_stories/21_52_3711_1_05.txt.

[56] David C. Lipscomb, "D.C. Officials Cautious on Legal Marijuana," Washington Times, December 10, 2009.

[57] Representative Barr (GA). "Amendment offered by Mr. Barr of Georgia." Congressional Record, 105th Congress, 1st Sess., September 17, 1997, p. H7388.

[58] "Medical Marijuana Now Legal." Tim Craig. D.C. Wire, Washington Post. July27, 2010. http:/voices.washingtonpost.com/dc/2010/07/medical_marijuana_now_legal.html.   "Liquor regulators may help oversee D.C. medical marijuana program." Mike DeBonis. Washington Post. August 7, 2010. http://www.washingtonpost.com/wp-dyn/content/article/2010/08/06/AR2010080606308_pf..html.   http://www.nbcwashington.com/news/local-beat/Medical-Marijuana-Makes-It-Into-Law-in-the-District.html.

[59] Wade, Jerry, "A Comparison of Medical Marijuana Programs in California and Oregon." *Alternatives Magazine*, Fall, 2006, Issue 39.

[60] "Medical Pot Dispensaries Under Scrutiny." Sandy Mazza. *San Gabrielle Valley Tribune*. February 15, 2007.

[61] "L.A.'s Marijuana Stores Take Root." William M. Welch, *USA Today*. March 8, 2007.

[62] "Pot-Friendly California: Amsterdam in America?" Richard Gonzales, npr, August 13, 2009. http://www.npr.org/templates/story/story.php?storyId=111784495&ps=rs.

[63] Dinkelspiel, Frances, "Berkeley Cannabis Collectives Slapped With Huge Tax Bills." Berkeleyside. February 3, 2011. Retrieved from http://www.berkeleyside.com/2011/02/03/berkeley-cannabis-collectives-slapped-with-hugetax-bills/

[64] Chairman Jerome E. Horton, California State Board of Equalization. (2010, February 3). *Tax Board Vice Chairperson Jerome Horton Proposes Taxing Marijuana Manufacturers* [Press Release]. Retrieved from http://www.boe.ca.gov/news/2010/16-10-H.pdf

[65] Dinkelspiel, Frances, "Berkeley Cannabis Collectives Slapped With Huge Tax Bills." Berkeleyside. February 3, 2011. Retrieved from http://www.berkeleyside.com/2011/02/03/berkeley-cannabis-collectives-slapped-with-hugetax-bills/

[66] U.S. Drug Enforcement Administration. (2008, May 16). *Modesto Marijuana Collective Owners Convicted* [Press Release]. Retrieved from http://www.justice.gov/dea/pubs/states/newrel/sanfran051608.html

[67] Korn, Peter, "Medical marijuana: a broken system." Portland Tribune. April 25, 2010.

[68] Jacklet, Ben "Marijuana goes mainstream in Southern Oregon," Oregon Business, May 2010. p 35.

[69] Ibid.

[70] Thurstone, Christian, "Smoke and mirrors: Colorado teenagers and marijuana." Denver Post, February 1, 2010. http://www.denverpost.com.opinion/ci_14289807?source=email.

[71] "Medical pot laws result in increased teen drug use." White Mountain Independent. January 15, 2011. http://www.wmicentral.com/news/latests_news/medical-pot-laws-result-in-increased-teen-drug-use/article-a6622a0c-1f42-11e0-a38e-001cc4c002e0.html.

[72] "AP Enterprise: Docs help make pot available in CA." November 1, 2010. http://www.cbs8.com/Global/story.asp?S=13423097

[73] "Much Better Choices than Marijuana for Medical Uses." Jeff Stone, Doctor of Pharmacology. *North County Times*. February 23, 2006.

[74] "Renters turn Brevard homes into pot farms." January 11, 2010. http://www.floridatoday.com/aricle/20100111/NEWS01/1110315?Renters-turn-Brevard-homes-into-pot-famrs-%7cvideo.

[75] "Vendors Reefer Sadness," Eric Bailey. *Los Angeles Times*. December 27, 2006.

[76] "City Reconsiders Pot Ban." Claudia Reed. *The Willits News*. October 27, 2006. http://www.willitsnews.com/localnews/ci_4561613.

[77] Marijuana 'grow houses' are creating problems in Arcata, California." *Los Angeles Times*, May 31, 2008. http://www.latimes.com/news/local/la-me-pot31-2008may31,0,2034882.story.

[78] Ibid.

[79] Move over meth: Marijuana 'grow houses' an increasing menace." MSN Real Estate. January 3, 2011. http://realestate.msn.com/article.aspx?cp-documentid=26924092.

[80] "Marijuana grows involved water diversion; Fish and Game called in". Tiffany Revelle. The Daily Journal. October 13, 2010. http://www.ukiahdaily.journal.com/fdcp?1287008819062.

[81] "Educators see rise in student drug use, blame medical marijuana." Great Falls Tribune, May 30, 2010. http://www.greatfallstribune.com/article/20100530/NEWS01/5300301/Educators-see-rise-in-student-drug-use-blamemedical-marijuana.

[82] "Owner of six L.A. -area medical marijuana dispensaries is arrested." *Los Angeles Times*, May 28, 2008. http://www.latimes.com/news/local/la-me-medpot28-2008may28,0,6101689.story.

83 "The Great California Weed Rush: How Medical Marijuana is Turning L.A. Pot Dealers into Semilegit Businessmen – No Beeper Required." Vanessa Grigoridias. *Rolling Stone Magazine*. February 7, 2007.
84 "Santa Cruz Pot Users, Sellers, Find Loopholes in State's Medical Marijuana Laws." Shanna McCord. *Santa Cruz Sentinel*. January 28, 2007.
85 "Teens at California School Getting High on Medical Marijuana." *KNSD-TV*, March 10, 2007.
86 "A Primer on Selling Pot Legally in California." Andrew Glazer. Associated Press. March 10, 2007.
87 "The Great California Weed Rush: How Medical Marijuana is Turning L.A. Pot Dealers into Semilegit Businessmen – No Beeper Required." Vanessa Grigoridias. *Rolling Stone Magazine*. February 7, 2007.
88 "Santa Cruz Pot Users, Sellers, Find Loopholes in State's Medical Marijuana Laws." Shanna McCord. *Santa Cruz Sentinel*. January 28, 2007.
89 "Drug overdose: Medical marijuana facing a backlash." The Associated Press, May 21, 2010. http://www.msnbc.com/id/37282436.
90 Ibid.
91 "Montana and Other States Struggle to Contain Medical Marijuana Boom, Related Violence." Medical News Today, May 27, 2010. http://www.medicalnewstoday.com/articles/190074. hph.
92 "Educators see rise in student drug use, blame medical marijuana." Great Falls Tribune, May 30, 2010. http://www.greatfallstribune.com/article/20100530/NEWS01/5300301/Educators-see-rise-in-student-drug-use-blamemedical-marijuana.
93 Ibid.
94 "Great Falls bans medical marijuana businesses outright." Richard Ecke. Great Falls Tribune. June 2, 2010. http://www.gratfallstribune.com/article/20100602/NEWS01/6020302/Geat-Falls-bans-medical-marijuana-businessesoutright.
95 "Cannabis Caravans Fuel Medical Pot Boom." Matt Volz. June 3, 2010. http://www.msnbc.com/id/37494656/ns/health-alternative_medicine/.
96 Ibid.
97 "Montana Board Bans Video Exams for Medical Marijuana." November 20, 2010. http://www.flatheadbeacon.com/articles/article/montana_board_bans_video_exams_for_medical_marijuana/20735/.
98 "Ritter signs bill regulating medical-marijuana industry." John Ingold. Denver Post. June 8, 2010. http://www.denverpost.com/ci_15248235.
99 Colorado official works to regulate, legitimize medical marijuana industry. Michael W. Savage. The Washington Post. July 25, 2010. http://www.washingtonpost,com/wp-dyn/content/article/2010/07/24/AR2010072402559_pf.html.
100 "Don't call it pot; it's "medicine" now. Dealers are caregivers, and buyers are patients…How Marijuana Got Mainstreamed.: Andrew Ferguson. Time Magazine. November 11, 2010. http://www.time.com/nation/article/0,8599,2030768,00.html.
101 "Colorado Medical Marijuana: State Supreme Court Rejects Challenge to Regulation." Huffington Post. January 11, 2011. http://www.huffingtonpost.com/2011/01/11/colorado-medical-marijuan_6_n_807444.html.
102 "Pruning pot spots." Editorial, July 30, 2009. http://www.latimes.com/news/opinion/la-ed-marijuana30-2009jul30,0,5752313.story .
103 "DA, DEA, US Attorney, IRS, Sheriff, SDPD Serve Warrants at Illegal Marijuana Dispensaries." Press Release, Office of the District Attorney, County of San Diego, September 10, 2009.
104 "L.A. submits new draft ordinance on medical marijuana." John Hoeffel, November 14, 2009. http://www.latimes.com/news/local/la-me-pot14-2009nov14,0,6360273.story.
105 D.A. chides L.A. Council, says he'll target pot dispensaries." John Hoeffel, LA Times, November 18, 2009. http://www.latimes.com/news/local/la-me-medical-marijuana18-2009nov18,0,5278631.story.

[106] "Judge proposes injunction on sales of pot at Eagle Rock dispensary." John Hoeffel, LA Times, December 2, 2009. http://www.latimes.com/news/local/la-me-medical-marijuana2-2009dec02,0,1,1283296.

[107] Richard Gonzales, "Los Angeles Officials Crack Down on Pot Clinics." NPR. February 25, 2010.

[108] "Los Angeles City Council passes medical marijuana dispensary ordinance." John Hoeffel, Los Angeles Times, January 19, 2010. http://www.latimes.com/news/local/la-me-medical-marijuana20-2010jan20,0,6270825.story.

[109] "LA orders 439 medical marijuana dispensaries to close." John Hoeffel, Los Angels Times, May 5, 2010. http://www.latimkes.com/news/local/la-me-0505-medical-marijuana-20100505,0,7354914.story.

[110] "Marijuana Hotbed Retreats on Medicinal Use." The New York Times. June 9, 2008. http://www.nytimes.com/2008/06/09us/09pot.html.

[111] Americans for Safe Access, January 21, 2011. http://www.safeaccess.org/article/php?id=3165.

[112] "California's Awash in 'legal' Marijuana," Bill O'Reilly, Post Bulletin. March 27, 2007.

[113] "New Report Finds Highest Levels of THC in U.S. Marijuana to Date." Office of National Drug Control Policy Press Release. May 14, 2009.

[114] "Study Finds Highest Levels of THC in U.S. Marijuana to Date: 20 Year Analysis of Marijuana Seizures Reveals a Doubling in Pot Potency Since Mid-80's." Office of National Drug Control Policy Press Release. April 25, 2007.

[115] "Teenage Schizophrenia Is the Issue, Not Legality." Robin Murray. Independent on Sunday. March 18, 2007. www.independent.co.uk.

[116] "The Debate Over the Drug is No Longer about Liberty. It's about Health." Antonio Maria Costa. March 27, 2007. Independent on Sunday, United Kingdom.

[117] "Why Marijuana Legalization Would Compromise Public Health and Safety." ONDCP Director Gil Kerlikowske, Speech Delivered at the California Police Chiefs Association Conference. March 4, 2010.

[118] "Nearly One in Ten First-Year College Students at One University Have a Cannabis Use Disorder; At-Risk Users Report Potentially Serious Cannabis-Related Problems." CESAR FAX, Vol. 17, Issue 3, January 21, 2008. www.cesar.umd.edu.

[119] "Teen Marijuana Use Worsens Depression: An Analysis of Recent Data Shows "Self Medication" Could Actually Make Things Worse." Office of National Drug Control Policy, May 2008. http://www.whitehousedrugpolicy.gov/news/press08/marij_mental_health.pdf.

[120] "Marijuana Links with Psychosis." AM with Tony Eastley. February 8, 2011. http://www.abc.nte.au/am/content/2011/s3132596.htm.

[121] "Cannabis increases risk of psychosis in teens." Telegraph News, June 2, 2008. http://www.telegraph.co.uk/news/uknews/2063199/Cannabis-increases-risk-of-psychosis-in-teens.html.

[122] "Marijuana May Shrink Parts of the Brain." Steven Reinberg. U.S. News and World Report – Online. June 2, 2008. http://health.usnews.com/articles/healthday/2008/06/02/marijuana_may_shrink_parts_of_the_brain.html. "Long-term Cannabis Users May Have Structural Brain Abnormalities." Science Daily. June 3, 2008. http://www.sciencedaily.com/releases/2008/06/080602160845.htm.

[123] Kate Benson, "Dope smokers not so mellow." The Sydney Morning Herald, July 30, 2009. http://www.smh.com/au/news/health/dope-smokers-not-so-mellow-20090407-9yOi.html.

[124] "Prenatal Marijuana Exposure and Intelligence Test Performance at Age 6." Abstract, Journal of the American Academy of Child & Adolescent Psychiatry. 47(3):254-263, March 2008. Goldschmidt, Lidush Ph.D. et al.

[125] "A Functional MRI Study of the Effects of Cannabis on the Brain." Prof. Phillip McGuire, UK, May 1, 2007. 2nd International Cannabis and Mental Health Conference, London, UK.

[126] "Study: Marijuana may Affect Neuron Firing." November 29, 2006. UPI.

[127] Laucius, Joanne. "Journal Articles Link Marijuana to Schizophrenia" August 28, 2006 www.Canada.com

[128] "Memory, Speed of Thinking and Other Cognitive Abilities Get Worse Over Time With Marijuana Use" March 15, 2006. http://www.news-medical.net

[129] "Drug Abuse; Drug Czar, Others Warn Parents that Teen Marijuana Use Can Lead to Depression." *Life Science Weekly.* May 31, 2005.

[130] Kearney, Simon. "Cannabis is Worst Drug for Psychosis." *The Australian.* November 21, 2005.

[131] Curtis, John. "Study Suggests Marijuana Induces Temporary Schizophrenia-Like Effects." *Yale Medicine.* Fall/Winter 2004.

[132] "Neurotoxicology; Neurocognitive Effects of Chronic Marijuana Use Characterized." *Health & Medicine Week.* 16 May 2005.

[133] "Teenage Schizophrenia is the Issue, Not Legality." Robin Murray. *Independent on Sunday.* March 18, 2007. www.independent.co.uk.

[134] "UN Warns of Cannabis Dangers as it Backs 'IoS' Drugs 'Apology'." Jonathan Owen. *Independent on Sunday.* March 25, 2007. www.independent.co.uk. and "Cannabis-related Schizophrenia Set to Rise, Say Researchers." *Science Daily.* March 26, 2007. www. sciencedaily.com/releases/2007/03/070324132832.htm.

[135] "Long-term pot use can double risk of psychosis." March 1, 2010. http://www.msnbc.com/id/ 35642202/ns/healthaddictions/?ns=health-addictions. Also McGrath J, et al "Association between cannabis use and psychosis-related outcomes using sibling pair analysis in a cohort of young adults" Arch Gen Psych 2010; DOI: 10.1001/archgenspychiatry.2010.6.

[136] "Quitting Pot Important Part of Trudeau's Recovery." Denise Ryan, *Vancouver Sun*, February 12, 2007.

[137] "Marijuana Use Affects Blood Flow in Brain Even After Abstinence." *Science Daily*, February 12, 2005. www.sciencedaily.com/releases/2005/02/050211084701.htm; *Neurology*, February 8, 2005, 64.488-493.

[138] "Marijuana Use Takes Toll on Adolescent Brain Function, Research Finds." Science Daily, October 15, 2008. http://www.scienedaily.com/releases/2008/10/081014111156.htm.

[139] State of California, Environmental Protection Agency, Office of Environmental Health Hazard Assessment, Safe Drinking Water and Toxic Enforcement Act of 1986, "Chemicals Known to the State to Cause Cancer or Reproductive Toxicity, September 11, 2009. http:// www.oehha.ca.gov/prop65_list/files/P65single091001.pdf.

[140] "Pot smoking during pregnancy may stunt fetal growth." January 22, 2010. http://www. reuters.com/article/id=Ustre60L55L20100122.

[141] "Heavy Marijuana Use Linked to Gum Disease, Study Shows." Science Daily, February 6, 2008. http://www.sciencedaily.com/releases/2008/02/080205161239.htm.; "Cannabis Smoking and Periodontal Disease Among Young Adults." *The Journal of the American Medical Association*, Vol. 299, No. 5, February 6, 2008. http://www.jama.ama-assn.org/ cgi/content/full/299/5/25.

[142] "Marijuana Smokers Face Rapid Lung Destruction – As Much As 20 Years Ahead of Tobacco Smokers." *Science Daily,* January 27, 2008. http://www.sciencedaily.com/releases/2008/ 01/080123104017.htm., "Bullous Lung Disease Due to Marijuana." *Respirology* (2008) 13, 122-127.

[143] Marijuana Smoke Contains Higher Levels of Certain Toxins Than Tobacco Smoke." *Science Daily*, December 18, 2007. http://sciencedaily.com/releases/2007/12/071217110328.htm. "A Comparison of Mainstream and Sidestream Marijuana and Tobacco Smoke Produced Under Two Machine Smoking Conditions." *American Chemical Society, Chemical Research in Toxicology*, December 17, 2008.

[144] "Marijuana Worsens COPD Symptoms in Current Cigarette Smokers." American Thoracic Society. *Science Daily*, May 23, 2007.

[145] "How Smoking Marijuana Damages the Fetal Brain." Karolinska Institute. *Science Daily*, May 29, 2007.

[146] "Cannabis Linked to Lung Cancer Risk." Martin Johnston. *New Zealand Herald*, March 27, 2007.

[147] "Marijuana Use Linked to Increased Risk of Testicular Cancer." Science Daily, February 9, 2009. http://www.scienedaily.com/releases/2009/02/090209075631.htm

[148] Department of Health and Human Services, Substance Abuse and Mental Health Services Administration, Center for Behavioral Health Statistics and Quality. "Highlights of the 2009 Drug Abuse Warning Network (DAWN), Findings on Drug-related Emergency Department Visits." December 2010. P. 3.

[149] Ibid. p.3.

[150] "A Day in the Life of American Adolescents: Substance Use Facts Update." OAS Report, April 29, 2010. http://www.oas.samhsa.gov.

[151] Tertrault, Jeannette M. MD, et. al., "Effects of Marijuana Smoking on Pulmonary Function Respiratory Complications: A Systematic Review" Arch. Intern. Med. 2007:167:221-228; Science Daily, "Long-term Marijuana Smoking Leads to Respiratory Complaints," www.sciencedaily.com/releases/2007/02/070212184119.htm.

[152] "Marijuana Use Linked to Early Bladder Cancer." http://www.medicalnewstoday.com/articlces/36695.php. January 26, 2006.

[153] "Marijuana Tied to Precancerous Lung Changes" Reuters. July 13, 2006. http://today.reuters.com/misc See also: "The Association Between Marijuana Smoking and Lung Cancer" Archives of Internal Medicine. http://archinte.ama.assn.org/cgi/content/full/166/12/1359?maxtoshow July 10, 2006.

[154] "Cannabis More Toxic than Cigarettes: Study," French National Consumers' Institute, 60 Million Consumers (magazine) April 2006, www.theage.com.au.

[155] "Conception and Pregnancy Put at risk by Marijuana Use" News-Medical.Net August 2, 2006 See also: "Fatty Acid Amide Hydrolase Deficiency Limits Earl Pregnancy Events" Research Article. Journal of Clinical Investigation. Published March 22, 2006, revised May 23, 2006 http://www.jci.org/cgi/content/full/116/8/2122

[156] In utero Marijuana Exposure Alters Infant Behavior. Reuters, January 17, 2007.

[157] Metro, Michael J., MD. "Association Between Marijuana Use and the Incidence of Transitional Cell Carcinoma Suggested" http://www.news.medical.net June 28, 2006.

[158] Tashkin, D.P., "Smoked Marijuana is a Cause of Lung Injury." Monaldi Archives for Chest Disease 63(2):93-100, 2005.

[159] "Marijuana Associated with Same Respiratory Symptoms as Tobacco," YALE News Release. January 13, 2005. <http://www.yale.edu/opa/newsr/05-01-13-01.all.htm> (14 January 2005). See also, "Marijuana Causes Same Respiratory Symptoms as Tobacco," January 13, 2005, 14WFIE.com.

[160] "What Americans Need to Know about Marijuana," page 9, ONDCP.

[161] "Decreased Respiratory Symptoms in Cannabis Users Who Vaporize," Harm Reduction Journal 4:11, April 16, 2007.

[162] "Marijuana Affects Brain Long-Term, Study Finds." Reuters. February 8, 2005. See also: "Marijuana Affects Blood Vessels." BBC News. 8 February 2005; "Marijuana Affects Blood Flow to Brain." The Chicago Sun-Times. February 8, 2005; Querna, Elizabeth. "Pot Head." US News & World Report. February 8, 2005.

[163] Smith, Michael. Medpage Today. February 12, 2007. http://www.medpagetoday.com/Neurology.GeneralNeurology/tb/5048.

[164] "HIV Patients: Marijuana Eases Foot Pain." Associated Press. February 13, 2007.

[165] Weiss, Rick. "Research Supports Medicinal Marijuana." Washington Post. February 13, 2007.

[166] Dahlbert, Carrie Peyton. "Marijuana Can Ease HIV-related Nerve Pain." McClatchy Newspapers. Feb. 13, 2007.

[167] Hashibe M, Morgenstem H, Cui Y, et al. Marijuana use and the risk of lung and upper aerodigestive tract cancers: results of a population-based case-control study. Cancer Epidemiol Biomarkers Prev 2006; 15:1829-1834.

[168] "Heavy marijuana use not linked to lung cancer," News-Medical.Net, Wednesday, May 24, 2006.

[169] http://www.nida.nih.gov/DirReports/DirRep207/DirectorReport8.html.

[170] http://www.umich.edu/news/index.html?Releases/2006/Oct06/r101006a.

[171] Harding, Anne. "Pot May Indeed Lead to Heroin Use, Rat Study Shows" *Reuters.* July 12, 2006. See also: "Why Teenagers Should Steer Clear of Cannabis" Vine, Gaia. www.New Scientist.com

[172] "What Americans Need to Know about Marijuana." *Office of National Drug Control Policy.* October 2003.

[173] Gfroerer, Joseph C., et al. "Initiation of Marijuana Use: Trends, Patterns and Implications." *Department of Health and Human Services, Substance Abuse and Mental Health Services Administration, Office of Applied Studies.* July 2002. Page 71.

[174] "Non-Medical Marijuana II: Rite of Passage or Russian Roulette?" *CASA Reports.* April 2004. Chapter V, Page 15.

[175] *The National Center on Addiction and Substance Abuse at Columbia University*, "Wasting the Best and the Brightest: Substance Abuse at America's Colleges and Universities." March 2007. page 4.

[176] "What Americans Need to Know about Marijuana," page 9, *ONDCP.*

[177] *Department of Health and Human Services, Substance Abuse and Mental Health Services Administration, Office of Applied Studies* ".Results from the 2009 National Survey on Drug Use and Health: Vol. I. Summary of National Findings." September 2010. Page 27.

[178] Ibid.

[179] Ibid.

[180] Ibid. p.54.

[181] "A Day in the Life of American Adolescents: Substance Use Facts Update." OAS Report, April 29, 2010. http://www.oas.samhsa.gov.

[182] Furber, Matt. "Threat of Meth—'the Devil's Drug'—increases." *Idaho Mountain Express and Guide.* December 28, 2005.

[183] "Medical pot laws result in increased teen drug use."White Mountain Independent. January 13, 2011. http://www.wmicentral.com/news/atests_news/medical-pot-laws-result-in-increased-teen-drug-use/article_a6622a0c-1f42-11e0-a38e-001cc4c002e0.html.

[184] "New Study shows dramatic shifts in substance abuse treatment admissions among states between 1998 and 2008." Department of Health and Human Services, Substance Abuse and Mental Health Administration, Office of Applied Studies. Press Release. December 22, 2010. http://www.samhsa.gov.

[185] California No. 1 in marijuana admissions." Cheryl Wetzstein. The Washington Times. December 30, 2010. http://www.washingtontimes.com/news/2010/dec/30/

[186] "Marijuana Myths & Facts: The Truth Behind 10 Popular Misperceptions." *Office of National Drug Control Policy.* <http://www.whitehousedrugpolicy.gov/publications/marijuana_myths_facts/index.html> (January 12, 2006).

[187] *Department of Health and Human Services, Substance Abuse and Mental Health Services Administration, Office of Applied Studies. "Results from the 2009 National Survey on Drug Use and Health: Vol. I. Summary of National Findings."* September 2009, page 1.

[188] "Early Marijuana Use Related to Later Illicit Drug Abuse and Dependence." CESARFAX. Vol. 19, Issue 41. October 25, 2010. www.cesar.umd.edu.

[189] Ibid.

[190] *Department of Health and Human Services, Substance Abuse and Mental Health Services Administration, Office of Applied Studies."Treatment Episode Data Set (TEDS) 1998-2008, National Admissions to Substance Abuse Treatment Services".* April 2010 Page 1.Table 1.1. www.oas.samhsa.gov .

[191] "Psychotherapeutic Interventions for Cannabis Abuse" July 21, 2006 http://www.news-medical.net See also: Denis C, Lavie D, Fatseas M, Aurizcombe M. "Psychotherapeutic Interventions for Cannabis Abuse and/or Dependence in Outpatient Settings". *The Cochrane Collaboration.* http://www.cochrane.org/reviews/en/ab005336.html.

[192] *Department of Health and Human Services, Substance Abuse and Mental Health Services Administration, Office of Applied Studies.* "Results from the 2009 National Survey on Drug Use and Health: Vol. I. Summary of National Findings." September 2010. Page 74.

[193] *Department of Health and Human Services, Substance Abuse and Mental Health Services Administration, Office of Applied Studies.* "Treatment Episode Data Set (TEDS) 1998-2008. National Admissions to Substance Abuse Treatment Services." April 2010. Page 2. www.oas.samhsa.gov.

[194] Ibid. Page 3. Table. 3.4.

[195] "Non-Medical Marijuana III: Rite of Passage or Russian Roulette?" A CASA White Paper, June 2008. http://www.casacolumbia.org.

[196] "Early Marijuana Use a Warning Sign For Later Gang Involvement," *ONDCP press release*, June 19, 2007.

[197] "The Relationship Between Alcohol, Drug Use and Violence Among Students." Community Anti-Drug Coalitions of American (CADCA). www.cadca.org. *Pride Surveys*, (2006) Questionnaire report for grades 6-12: 2006 National Summary. Page 184. http://www.pridesurveys.com/customercetner/us05ns.pdf.

[198] *Office of National Drug Control Policy.* (2006) "Marijuana Myths and Facts: The Truth Behind 10 Popular Misperceptions. "Page 10. http://www.whitehousedrugpolicy.gov/publications/marijuana_mythis_facts.

[199] Ibid.

[200] NIDA InfoFacts: Drugged Driving, September 10, 2009, page 1. http://drugabuse.gov/Infofacts/driving.html.

[201] Volz, Matt. "Drug overdose: Medical marijuana facing a backlash." http://www.msnbc.msn.com/id/37282436.

[202] *Department of Health and Human Services, Substance Abuse and Mental Health Services Administration, Office of Applied Studies.* Results from the 2009 National Survey on Drug Use and Health: Vol. I. Summary of National Findings. September 2010. Page 28.

[203] "One-third of Fatally Injured Drivers with Known Test Results Tested Positive for at Least one Drug in 2009. CESARFAX. Vol. 19, Issue 49. December 20, 2010. www.cesar.umd.edu.

[204] Ibid.

[205] "Cannabis and Driving: A Scientific and Rational Review." Armentano, Paul. *NORML/NORML Foundation.* January 10, 2008. http://normal.org/index.cfm?Group_ID=7475 for article and http://normal.org/index.cfm?Group_ID=7459 for the full report.

[206] DuPont, Robert. "National Survey Confirms that Drugged Driving is Significantly More Widespread than Drunk Driving." Commentary, Institute for Behavior and Health, July 17, 2009. page 1. http://www.ibhinc.org.

[207] "Drug-Impaired Driving by Youth Remains Serious Problem." NIDA News Release, October 29, 2007. http://www.drugabuse.gov/newsroom/07/NR10-29.html.

[208] "The Drugged Driving Epidemic," *The Washington Post*, June 17, 2007.

[209] DuPont, Robert. "National Survey Confirms that Drugged Driving is Significantly More Widespread than Drunk Driving." Commentary, Institute for Behavior and Health, July 17, 2009. page 1. http://www..ibhinc.org.

[210] "Cannabis Almost Doubles Risk of Fatal Crashes". December 2005. BMJ.com. http://bmj.bmjjournals.com/content/vol331/issue7528/press_release.shtml.

[211] Drummer, OH, Gerostamoulos J, Batziris H, Chu M, Caplehorn J, Robertson MD, Swann P. "The Involvement of drugs in drivers of motor vehicles killed in Australian road traffic crashes.." Accid Anal Prev 36(2):229-48, 2004.

[212] "Drug-Driving Test Kits Get Green Light" *Scotland on Sunday*, September 9, 2006. http://www.mapinc.org/tlcnews/v06/n1013/a05.htm?134.

[213] "Drugged Driving Poses Serious Safety Risk to Teens; Campaign to Urge Teens to 'Steer Clear of Pot' During National Drunk and Drugged Driving (3D) Prevention Month." *PR Newswire*. December 2, 2004.

[214] Couper, Fiona, J, and Logan, Barry *Drugs and Human Performance Fact Sheets* National Highway Traffic Safety Administration., page 11. April 2004.

[215] "Pot Smoking Linked to Crash." Las Vegas Review-Journal. July 18, 2008. http://www.lvrj.com/news/25610594.html.

[216] "Police: Man Was High on Pot When Car Fatally Stuck Woman." April 20, 2010. http://www.msnbc.com/id/36669052/from/ET/.

[217] "Marijuana Blamed in Fatal Crash. *The Patriot News*. May 1, 2007.

[218] "Ind. Teen Charged in Deadly Car Crash. *The New York Times*. August 2, 2006.

[219] Maddux, Stan. "Teen Whose Car Hit Bus Allegedly on Marijuana." Post-trib.com. August 24, 2006. http://www.post-trib.com/cgi-bin/pto-story/news/zl/08-24-06_zl_news_15.html

[220] "Nation: Drug Test Positive for Driver in Deadly Crash." *Orange County Register*. May 14, 1999.

[221] Edmondson, Aimee. "Drug Tests Required of Child Care Drivers – Fatal Crash Stirs Change; Many Already Test Positive." *The Commercial Appeal*. July 2, 2003.

[222] McDonald, Melody and Boyd, Deanna. "Jury Gives Mallard 50 Years for Murder; Victim's Son Forgives but Says 'Restitution is Still Required.'" *Fort Worth Star Telegram*. June 28, 2003.

[223] "Boy, 8, Who Was Struck While Riding Bike Dies." *The Dallas Morning News*, April 25, 2005.

[224] The Associated Press. "Police: Driver in Fatal Crash had Drugs in System." *The Associated Press*. June 1, 2003.

[225] "New pot law blamed as violence escalates." Laurel J. Sweet and O'Ryan Johnson. Boston Herald. November 15, 2010. http://www.bostonherald.com/news/politics/view.bg?Articleid=1296392.

[226] "FHP: Man led trooper on chase with kids-and pot – in car." Bay News 9. February 3, 2011. http://www.baynews9.com/article/news/2011/february/204034/FHP:-Man-led-trooper-on-chase-with-kids-in-car-?cid=rss.

[227] "Driving under influence of marijuana a growing problems." Gwen Florio. Missoulian.com January 16, 2011. http://missoulian.com/news/local/article_1d9f6f8a-2137-11e0-a0be-001cc4c002e0.html.

[228] "Jessica Gamble, Ohio Mom, Charged for Teaching 2-Year-Old Daughter to Smoke Marijuana." Caroline Black. CBS WKRC. September 16, 2010. http://www.cbsnews.com/8301-504083_162-20016662-504083.html.

[229] "Va. Pair Charged After Toddler Eats Marijuana." Whz.com. October 8, 2010. http://wjz.com/wireapnewsva/Manassas.pair.charged.2.1953794.html.

[230] "Video shows parents giving pot pipe to toddler." Beatriz Valenzuela. Daily Press. January 17, 2011. http://www.vvdailypress.com/articles/parents-25426-pipe.pot.html.

[231] "Police: Mom gave pot to her 3 kids." Lance Berry. October 28, 2010. http://www.wcpo.com/dpp/news/region/_east_cincinnati/madisonville/police%3A-mom-gave-pot-to-3-kids.

[232] "Toddler in Critical Condition After Ingesting Marijuana." February 2, 2011. http://losangeles.cbslocal.com/2011/02/02/toddler-in-critical-condition-after-ingesting-marijuana.

[233] "Mother charged after toddler hospitalized for eating marijuana, pills." Michelle Hunter. The Times-Picayune. October 13, 2008. http://www.nola.com/news/index.ssf/2008/10children_3_and_4_hospitalized. html.

[234] "Police: Criminal targeting San Jose's medicinal marijuana clubs." Sean Webby. The Mercury News. December 16, 2010. http://www.mercurynews.com/fdcp?1293042861859.

[235] "LAPD investigates third shooting at a medical marijuana dispensary." Andrew Blackstein, Los Angeles Times, July 1, 2010. http://www.latimes.com/news/local/la-me-pot-shooting-201000701,0,4009176.story.

[236] "Pentagon shooter had a history of mental illness." March 5, 2010. http://www.msnbc.com/id/35716821/ns/us_news_crime_and_courts/

[237] Parents warned police of Pentagon shooter's bizarre mental state." Washington Post. March 5, 2010.   http://www.washingtonpost.com/wp-dyn/cotnent/article/2010/03/05/ AR2010030500957_2.html?hpid=dynamiclead.

[238] "Calif. Drug dealer guilty of murdering 15-year-old." San Diego Union Tribune, July 9, 2008. www.sandiego.com.

[239] "Lawyer Who Fell to Death…Was Driven Mad by Cannabis." Daily Mail, May 15, 2007.

[240] The Associated Press. "Murder Charges Filed in Blaze that Killed Two Firefighters." The Associated Press. August 21, 2004.

[241] "Pilot Used Marijuana before Fatal Plane Crash." ABC Newsonline. February 7, 2006. www. abc.net.au/news/newsitems/200602/s1564190.htm.

[242] "4 charged in Chaska Slaying." David Hanners. Pioneer Press. January 13, 2006. http://www. twincities.com.

[243] "NTSB: Pilot Had Marijuana In His System." KTHV Little Rock. February 6, 2006. www. todaysthv.com.

[244] U.S. Sentencing Commission, "2008 Sourcebook of Federal Sentencing Statistics,: see: http://www.ussc.gov/ANNRPT/2008/SBTOC08.htm, Table 33.

[245] Bureau of Justice Statistics, "Drug Use and Dependence", State and Federal Prisoners, 2004, October 2006.

[246] United States Sentencing Commission, "2006 Sourcebook of Federal Sentencing Statistics," June 2007.

[247] Ibid.

[248] Office of National Drug Control Policy. "Who's Really in Prison for Marijuana?" May 2005 Page 22.

[249] "New study Reveals Scope of Drug and Crime Connection: As Many as 87 Percent of People Arrested for Any Crime Test Positive for Drug Use." Office of National Drug Control Policy Press Release, May 28, 2009 and Fact Sheet 2008 ADAM II Report, www. whitehousedrugpolicy.gov.

[250] Angus Reid Global Monitor, Polls & Research, December 23, 2006. www.angus-reid.com/ polls/index.cfm.fuseaction/viewItem/itemID/14189.

[251] European Monitoring Centre for Drugs and Drug Addiction, "2008 Annual Report: The State of the Drug Problem in Europe." Office of Official Publications of the European Communities, Luxembourg, June 2008, page 11. see also www.emcdda.europea.eu.

[252] "Europe faces new challenges posed by changes in drug supply and use." European Monitoring Centre for Drugs and Drug Addiction, Annual Report 2010: Highlights. October 11, 2010. www.emcdda.europa.eu.

[253] "Liberal-National Government to overturn soft-on-drugs legislation." Government Media Office, Ministerial Media Statements, Government of Western Australia, October 11, 2009. http://www.mediastatements.wa.gov.au.

[254] "Australia: Doc Group Lobbies for Tougher Western Australia Marijuana Laws, Cites Mental Health Threat." May 24, 2008. The Western Australia. http://www.thewest.com/au/default. aspx?MenuID=158&ContentID=74974.

[255] "Warning Marijuana is 'Not a Soft Drug," Australian Associated Press. August 1, 2006. http://www.theage.com.au/news/National/Warning-marijuana-is-not-a-soft-drug/2006.

[256] Burman, John. "Ontario Toughens Rules to Uproot Grow-ops" The Hamilton Spectator, August 4, 2006 http://www.hamiltonspectator.comNASAPP/cs/ContentServer?pagename= hamilton/Layout See also: CTV Toronto, August 3, 2006.

[257] Adlaf, Edward M. and Paglia-Boak, Angela, Center for Addiction and Mental Health, Drug Use Among Ontario Students, 1977-2005, CAMH Research Document Series No. 16. The study does not contain data on marijuana use among 12th graders prior to 1999. See also: Canadian Addiction Survey, Highlights (November 2004) and Detailed Report (March 2005), produced by Health Canada and the Canadian Executive Council on Addictions; Youth and Marijuana Quantitative Research' 2003 Final Report, Health Canada; Tibbetts,

Janice and Rogers, Dave. "Marijuana Tops Tobacco Among Teens, Survey Says: Youth Cannabis Use Hits 25-Year Peak," *The Ottawa Citizen*, October 29, 2003.
[258] Kleinhubbert, Guido. "Germany's 'McDope' Problem." *Spiegel Online*. 17, August 2006. http://www.service.spiegel.de/cache/international/spiegel/0,1518,432078,00.html.
[259] "Amsterdam Bans Smoking of Marijuana in Some Public Places." *Expatica's* January 29, 2007. www.expatica.com/actual/article.asp?subchannel_id=19&story_id-5804.
[260] *The New York Times*, August 20, 2006.
[261] "Cannabis Bars in Limburg to be for Members Only," NIS News Bulletin, May 13, 2009, see: http://www.nisnews.nl/public/103509_1.htm.
[262] "Amsterdam's cannabis-selling coffee shops face crackdown." Stanley Pignal. The Washington Post. October 8, 2010. http://www.washigntonpost.com/wp-dyn/content/article/2010/10/08/AR2010100806139_pf.html.
[263] "What Americans Need to Know about Marijuana," *ONDCP*, Page 10.
[264] Dutch Health, Welfare and Sports Ministry Report. April 23, 2004.
[265] INTRAVAL Bureau for Research & Consultancy. "Coffeeshops in the Netherlands 2004." *Dutch Ministry of Justice*. June 2005. <http://www.intraval.nl/en/b/b45.html>.
[266] Id.
[267] Collins, Larry. "Holland's Half-Baked Drug Experiment." *Foreign Affairs Vol. 73, No. 3*. May-June 1999: Pages 87-88.
[268] Hibell, B; Guttormsson, U, Ahlstrom, S, Balakireva, O., Bjarnason, T., Kokkevi, A., Kraus, L., "The 2007 ESPAD AReport-Substgance Use Among Students in 35 European Countries," the Swedish Council for information on Alcohol and Other Drugs (CAN), Stockholm, Sweden, 2009.
[269] "Netherlands from 12th to 5th Place in Europe on Cannabis Usage," NIS News Bulletin, April 4, 2009, see: http://www.nisnews.nl/public/040409_1.htm.
[270] European Monitoring Centre for Drugs and Drug Addiction, Situation Summary for Portugal, November 2010. http://www.emcdda,europa,eu/publications/country-overviews/pt.
[271] "Singapore Gives Treatment Option to Marijuana, Cocaine Users." *Drug War Chronicle, Issue 495, July 27, 2007.*
[272] "Swiss approve heroin scheme but vote down marijuana law." The Guardian, December 1, 2008. http://www.guardina.co.uk/world/2008/dec/01/switterland-drugs-herion/
[273] Cohen, Roger. "Amid Growing Crime, Zurich Closes a Park it Reserved for Drug Addicts." *The New York Times*. February 11, 1992.
[274] Ormston, Rachel, Bradshaw, Paul and Anderson, Simon, *Scottish Social Attitudes Survey 2009, Public Attitudes to Drugs and Drug Use in Scotland*, Scottish Government Social Research, 2010.Page 1.
[275] "UK: Cannabis To Be Reclassified As A Class B Drug." May 8, 2008. http://www.scoop.co.nz/stories/WO0805/S00105.htm.
[276] "Cannabis: An Apology." *The Independent on Sunday*. March 18, 2007. www.news.independent.co.uk/uk/health_medical/article2368994.ece.
[277] Koster, Olinka, Doughty, Steve, and Wright, Stephen. "Cannabis Climbdown." *Daily Mail (London)*. March 19, 2005. *See* also. Revill, Jo, and Bright, Martin. "Cannabis: the Questions that Remain Unanswered." *The Observer*. 20 March 2005; Steele, John and Helm, Toby. "Clarke Reviews "Too Soft" Law on Cannabis." *The Daily Telegraph (London)*. 19 March 2005; Brown, Colin. "Clarke Orders Review of Blunkett Move to Downgrade Cannabis." *The Independent (London)*. March 19, 2005.
[278] "Blair's 'Concern' on Cannabis." *The Irish Times*. May 4, 2005. *See also*, Russell, Ben. "Election 2005: Blair Rules Out National Insurance Rise." *The Independent (London)*. May 4, 2005.
[279] "Top U.S. and United Nations Anti-Drug Officials Warn About Increasing Threat of Marijuana." Press Release. June 26, 2006. *ONDCP*. http://www.whitehousedrugpolicy.gov/news/press/06/062606.html.

[280] Johnston, L.D., O'Malley. P.M., Bachman, J.G. & Schulenberg, J.E. (December 14, 2010.) "Marijuana use is rising: ecstasy use is beginning to rise; and alcohol use is declining among U.S. Teens." University of Michigan News Service, Ann Arbor, MI. December 14, 2010. http://www.monitoringthefuture.org.

[281] U.S. Department of Health and Human Services, National Institutes of Health, National Institute on Drug Abuse, "Teen marijuana use increase, especially among eighth-graders." Press Release, December 14, 2010.

[282] Department of Health And Human Services, Substance Abuse and Mental Health Services Administration, Office of Applied Studies, "Results From The 2009 National Survey On Drug Use And Health: Volume I. Summary of National Findings." September 2010. Pages 1-2.

[283] Ibid.p.65.

[284] Ibid.p.66.

[285] Partnership for a Drug Free America and the MetLife Foundation, *2009 Partnership Attitude Tracking Study*, March 2, 2010. http://www.drugfree.org

[286] DEA Domestic Cannabis Eradication/Suppression Program, 2009eradication season. This information can also be found at http://www.albany.edu/sourcebook/pdf//t4382009.pdf.

[287] Id.

In: The Medical Marijuana Question …   ISBN: 978-1-62417-080-5
Editors: C. Gable and M. Feuerstein   © 2013 Nova Science Publishers, Inc.

Chapter 3

INVESTIGATIONS AND PROSECUTIONS IN STATES AUTHORIZING THE MEDICAL USE OF MARIJUANA*

U.S. Department of Justice

MEMORANDUM FOR SELECTED UNITED STATES ATTORNEYS

This memorandum provides clarification and guidance to federal prosecutors in States that have enacted laws authorizing the medical use of marijuana. These laws vary in their substantive provisions and in the extent of state regulatory oversight, both among the enacting States and among local jurisdictions within those States. Rather than developing different guidelines for every possible variant of state and local law, this memorandum provides uniform guidance to focus federal investigations and prosecutions in these States on core federal enforcement priorities.

The Department of Justice is committed to the enforcement of the Controlled Substances Act in all States. Congress has determined that marijuana is a dangerous drug, and the illegal distribution and sale of marijuana is a serious crime and provides a significant source of revenue to large-scale criminal enterprises, gangs, and cartels. One timely example

---

* This is an edited, reformatted and augmented version of the Office of the Deputy Attorney General, dated October 19, 2009.

underscores the importance of our efforts to prosecute significant marijuana traffickers: marijuana distribution in the United States remains the single largest source of revenue for the Mexican cartels.

The Department is also committed to making efficient and rational use of its limited investigative and prosecutorial resources. In general, United States Attorneys are vested with "plenary authority with regard to federal criminal matters" within their districts. USAM 9-2.001. In exercising this authority, United States Attorneys are "invested by statute and delegation from the Attorney General with the broadest discretion in the exercise of such authority." *Id.* This authority should, of course, be exercised consistent with Department priorities and guidance.

The prosecution of significant traffickers of illegal drugs, including marijuana, and the disruption of illegal drug manufacturing and trafficking networks continues to be a core priority in the Department's efforts against narcotics and dangerous drugs, and the Department's investigative and prosecutorial resources should be directed towards these objectives. As a general matter, pursuit of these priorities should not focus federal resources in your States on individuals whose actions are in clear and unambiguous compliance with existing state laws providing for the medical use of marijuana. For example, prosecution of individuals with cancer or other serious illnesses who use marijuana as part of a recommended treatment regimen consistent with applicable state law, or those caregivers in clear and unambiguous compliance with existing state law who provide such individuals with marijuana, is unlikely to be an efficient use of limited federal resources. On the other hand, prosecution of commercial enterprises that unlawfully market and sell marijuana for profit continues to be an enforcement priority of the Department. To be sure, claims of compliance with state or local law may mask operations inconsistent with the terms, conditions, or purposes of those laws, and federal law enforcement should not be deterred by such assertions when otherwise pursuing the Department's core enforcement priorities.

Typically, when any of the following characteristics is present, the conduct will not be in clear and unambiguous compliance with applicable state law and may indicate illegal drug trafficking activity of potential federal interest:

- unlawful possession or unlawful use of firearms;
- violence;
- sales to minors;

- financial and marketing activities inconsistent with the terms, conditions, or purposes of state law, including evidence of money laundering activity and/or financial gains or excessive amounts of cash inconsistent with purported compliance with state or local law;
- amounts of marijuana inconsistent with purported compliance with state or local law;
- illegal possession or sale of other controlled substances; or
- ties to other criminal enterprises.

Of course, no State can authorize violations of federal law, and the list of factors above is not intended to describe exhaustively when a federal prosecution may be warranted. Accordingly, in prosecutions under the Controlled Substances Act, federal prosecutors are not expected to charge, prove, or otherwise establish any state law violations. Indeed, this memorandum does not alter in any way the Department's authority to enforce federal law, including laws prohibiting the manufacture, production, distribution, possession, or use of marijuana on federal property. This guidance regarding resource allocation does not "legalize" marijuana or provide a legal defense to a violation of federal law, nor is it intended to create any privileges, benefits, or rights, substantive or procedural, enforceable by any individual, party or witness in any administrative, civil, or criminal matter. Nor does clear and unambiguous compliance with state law or the absence of one or all of the above factors create a legal defense to a violation of the Controlled Substances Act. Rather, this memorandum is intended solely as a guide to the exercise of investigative and prosecutorial discretion.

Finally, nothing herein precludes investigation or prosecution where there is a reasonable basis to believe that compliance with state law is being invoked as a pretext for the production or distribution of marijuana for purposes not authorized by state law. Nor does this guidance preclude investigation or prosecution, even when there is clear and unambiguous compliance with existing state law, in particular circumstances where investigation or prosecution otherwise serves important federal interests.

Your offices should continue to review marijuana cases for prosecution on a case-by-case basis, consistent with the guidance on resource allocation and federal priorities set forth herein, the consideration of requests for federal assistance from state and local law enforcement authorities, and the Principles of Federal Prosecution.

cc: All United States Attorneys

Lanny A. Breuer
Assistant Attorney General
Criminal Division

B. Todd Jones
United States Attorney
District of Minnesota
Chair, Attorney General's Advisory Committee

Michele M. Leonhart
Acting Administrator
Drug Enforcement Administration

H. Marshall Jarrett
Director
Executive Office for United States Attorneys

Kevin L. Perkins
Assistant Director
Criminal Investigative Division
Federal Bureau of Investigation

In: The Medical Marijuana Question ...   ISBN: 978-1-62417-080-5
Editors: C. Gable and M. Feuerstein   © 2013 Nova Science Publishers, Inc.

Chapter 4

GUIDANCE REGARDING THE OGDEN MEMO IN JURISDICTIONS SEEKING TO AUTHORIZE MARIJUANA FOR MEDICAL USE[*]

U.S. Department of Justice

MEMORANDUM FOR UNITED STATE ATTORNEYS

Over the last several months some of you have requested the Department's assistance in responding to inquiries from State and local governments seeking guidance about the Department's position on enforcement of the Controlled Substances Act (CSA) in jurisdictions that have under consideration, or have implemented, legislation that would sanction and regulate the commercial cultivation and distribution of marijuana purportedly for medical use. Some of these jurisdictions have considered approving the cultivation of large quantities of marijuana, or broadening the regulation and taxation of the substance. You may have seen letters responding to these inquiries by several United States Attorneys. Those letters are entirely consistent with the October 2009 memorandum issued by Deputy Attorney General David Ogden to federal prosecutors in States that have enacted laws authorizing the medical use of marijuana (the "Ogden Memo").

---

[*] This is an edited, reformatted and augmented version of the Office of the Deputy Attorney General, dated June 29, 2011.

The Department of Justice is committed to the enforcement of the Controlled Substances Act in all States. Congress has determined that marijuana is a dangerous drug and that the illegal distribution and sale of marijuana is a serious crime that provides a significant source of revenue to large scale criminal enterprises, gangs, and cartels. The Ogden Memorandum provides guidance to you in deploying your resources to enforce the CSA as part of the exercise of the broad discretion you are given to address federal criminal matters within your districts.

A number of states have enacted some form of legislation relating to the medical use of marijuana. Accordingly, the Ogden Memo reiterated to you that prosecution of significant traffickers of illegal drugs, including marijuana, remains a core priority, but advised that it is likely not an efficient use of federal resources to focus enforcement efforts on individuals with cancer or other serious illnesses who use marijuana as part of a recommended treatment regimen consistent with applicable state law, or their caregivers. The term "caregiver" as used in the memorandum meant just that: individuals providing care to individuals with cancer or other serious illnesses, not commercial operations cultivating, selling or distributing marijuana.

The Department's view of the efficient use of limited federal resources as articulated in the Ogden Memorandum has not changed. There has, however, been an increase in the scope of commercial cultivation, sale, distribution and use of marijuana for purported medical purposes. For example, within the past 12 months, several jurisdictions have considered or enacted legislation to authorize multiple large-scale, privately-operated industrial marijuana cultivation centers. Some of these planned facilities have revenue projections of millions of dollars based on the planned cultivation of tens of thousands of cannabis plants.

The Ogden Memorandum was never intended to shield such activities from federal enforcement action and prosecution, even where those activities purport to comply with state law. Persons who are in the business of cultivating, selling or distributing marijuana, and those who knowingly facilitate such activities, are in violation of the Controlled Substances Act, regardless of state law. Consistent with resource constraints and the discretion you may exercise in your district, such persons are subject to federal enforcement action, including potential prosecution. State laws or local ordinances are not a defense to civil or criminal enforcement of federal law with respect to such conduct, including enforcement of the CSA. Those who engage in transactions involving the proceeds of such activity may also be in violation of federal money laundering statutes and other federal financial laws.

The Department of Justice is tasked with enforcing existing federal criminal laws in all states, and enforcement of the CSA has long been and remains a core priority.

cc: Lanny A. Breuer
     Assistant Attorney General, Criminal Division

     B. Todd Jones
     United States Attorney
     District of Minnesota
     Chair, AGAC

     Michele M. Leonhart
     Administrator
     Drug Enforcement Administration

     H. Marshall Jarrett
     Director
     Executive Office for United States Attorneys

     Kevin L. Perkins
     Assistant Director
     Criminal Investigative Division
     Federal Bureau of Investigations

INDEX

D

T

transport, 46
trauma, 70
treaties, 10
treatment, vii, viii, 1, 2, 4, 5, 25, 26, 27, 28,
    30, 34, 37, 41, 51, 52, 65, 66, 74, 75, 81,
    82, 97, 104, 108
trial, 19
tumor, 63
tumors, 61
twins, 64

U

U.S. Department of Agriculture, 49
UK, 56, 90, 94, 101
UN, 95
uniform, ix, 77, 103
United, vii, viii, x, 1, 3, 4, 8, 9, 10, 17, 19,
    20, 21, 22, 23, 25, 26, 30, 31, 33, 51, 52,
    65, 69, 70, 76, 82, 83, 86, 87, 89, 94,
    100, 101, 103, 104, 106, 107, 109
United Kingdom, 30, 52, 70, 83, 94
United Nations, 52, 87, 101
United States, vii, viii, x, 1, 3, 4, 8, 9, 10,
    17, 19, 20, 21, 22, 23, 25, 26, 31, 33, 51,
    52, 65, 69, 76, 82, 86, 89, 100, 104, 106,
    107, 109
universities, 64
unplanned pregnancies, 41
urban, 77
urine, 42, 60
USA, 92
uterus, 60

V

varieties, 87
vehicles, 98
verbal fluency, 55
veto, 17, 34, 91
victims, 61, 70

video games, 75
videotape, 73, 90
violence, 47, 73, 77, 99, 104
vision, 31
vomiting, 29, 30
vote, 32, 34, 35, 36, 101
voters, 32, 33, 34, 35, 36, 40, 46, 82, 91
voting, 86
vulnerable people, 54

W

war, 52
Washington, 17, 19, 20, 23, 32, 86, 89, 90,
    91, 93, 96, 97, 98, 100, 101
waste, 9
water, 43, 44, 78, 92
weapons, 45
welfare, 8
wellness, 91
Western Australia, 78, 100
Western countries, 87
wheezing, 61
White House, 67, 76
White Paper, 98
wholesale, 4, 31
wildlife, 44
wires, 43, 75
withdrawal, 66
withdrawal symptoms, 66
workers, 65
worldwide, 77
worry, 22

Y

Yale University, 54
yield, 12, 41, 43
young adults, 41, 56, 68, 95
young people, 41, 52, 53, 56, 64, 78, 79, 80,
    81, 84